Atlanta in 1890

"THE GATE CITY"

Atlanta in 1890

"THE GATE CITY"

*The Original 1890 Edition
with a New Introduction and Annotations
Republished by the Atlanta Historical Society
to Commemorate Its Sixtieth Anniversary*

Atlanta Historical Society
Atlanta, Georgia

Mercer University Press
Macon, Georgia
1986

ISBN 0-86554-241-4

The paper used in this publication meets
the minimum requirements of American National Standard
for Information Sciences—Permanence of Paper
for Printed Library Materials, ANSI Z39.48-1984.

Pages 1-91 and the photographs are reprinted as they appeared in the original 1890 edition,
published by the George B. Pratt Publishing Company and the Art Publishing Company,
both of Neenah, Wisconsin.

CONTENTS

PREFACE

$\mathcal{A}$TLANTA in 1890: "The Gate City" is published to commemorate the sixtieth anniversary of the founding of the Atlanta Historical Society. Committed to the study of Atlanta's past and to its preservation for future generations, the Society finds this volume a most fitting way to mark the occasion.

The reissuance of this very scarce work, which the Society hopes will make people even more aware of the early beauty and commerce of our city, has at least one short human interest story. This organization was donated an unbound copy of "The Gate City" as it was issued in its eleven parts. The copy came from a woman by the name of Joan Noone of Portsmouth, Rhode Island, whose grandmother had been married in Atlanta and had received the book as a wedding present. She wanted to make the volume a gift to the Society to assure it a good home where people might enjoy reading the work. This small publication project should assure both.

When the Atlanta Historical Society was founded in 1926, the city had experienced steady growth since the time "The Gate City" was published. Buildings were springing up downtown; suburbs were rapidly developing, but the area was undergoing nothing like the tenfold growth it would enjoy over the next half century. Walter McElreath and a small group of farsighted citizens banded together to petition for a corporation organized for purposes "purely literary, social and educational in character." They had no set meeting place and no staff. They did not begin to publish The Atlanta Historical Bulletin for more than a year. Yet in scarcely ten years they sought headquarters in the Biltmore Hotel and hired Miss Ruth Blair, state archivist, to be full-time executive secretary. In a few more years, they outgrew the Biltmore office. After subsequent moves to the Erlanger Hotel and a site on Peachtree Street, the Society finally, in 1966, purchased the Swan House, former home of Mrs. Edward H. Inman, and moved to Buckhead. Shortly thereafter a modern administration building, library, and gallery space opened, named appropriately for the same Walter McElreath who petitioned to found the Society and was its journal's first editor.

If that band of progressive citizens could see the Atlanta Historical Society today, they would marvel at their creation. Its numbers have grown from fourteen to almost four thousand. It has moved again to serve the downtown area, having as another anniversary event this year established a small downtown cultural information center and museum at 140 Peachtree Street. Its established headquarters to the north in Buckhead welcomes through its doors more than 100,000 visitors annually. They come to tour the museum galleries, the Swan House, the Tullie Smith Restoration complex, the twenty-six acres of lovely grounds. They come to the library and archives for historical research; to Woodruff Auditorium for lectures, films, music, and drama; to the Members' Room for seminars, discussions, and receptions; to the professional staff of the Society for information and advice as they pursue their diverse interests in the city.

It is with a great sense of pride and accomplishment in the past sixty years that we publish this volume today. Through it, scenes of the city at the end of the last century are again available to everyone. The Board of Trustees and the Publications Committee are to be commended for their foresight and interest in the project. For continuing support and efforts toward the publication, special credit is due the Watson Brown Foundation for sharing the costs of this work; historian Timothy Crimmins of Georgia State University for placing the book's genre in historical perspective; Library/Archives Director William A. Richards for annotating the photographs; AHS and City Historian Franklin Garrett for verifying the annotations; library/archives staff members Rosa Dickens, Donald Rooney, Anne Salter, and Nancy Wight for research to document the annotations; Director of Publications Jane Powers Weldon for editing and managing production; publications staff Matthew Pieper and Jo Crawford Phelps and AHS volunteer Alison Zimmerman for proofreading; the entire AHS staff for support functions; and finally Mercer University Press for fine efforts to bring the project to completion.

Perhaps this story of a city growing into a new century will inspire support for a similar project, Society sponsored, to record the more recent history of Atlanta before the particulars of the twentieth century are lost to the ages.

John Harlow Ott
Executive Director
The Atlanta Historical Society
Atlanta, Georgia
June 1986

INTRODUCTION TO *"THE GATE CITY"*

By Timothy J. Crimmins

"*T*HIS *publication is not* intended to be an historical work," begins the introductory paragraph of *"The Gate City";* rather, it is designed "to furnish in a work of art, a fair delineation of the city of Atlanta." Originally published in 1890, at the beginning of the city's second half century, *"The Gate City"* also had an eye on history because its illustrations were chosen "with a view of preserving for the future what might become of historic interest." With that in mind, the author of the text went on to speculate about what might make these photographs fascinating to future generations of Atlantans: "The passing years bring change to everything over which they take their flight, and whatever may be the destiny of this city it will be interesting in after years to look upon the features of former years" (page 1). Yes, it is most exciting to look back on the city of a hundred years ago. But what we are examining is not the city itself; it is an artistic rendering that freezes hundreds of moments and places in a vital, complex, and changing town in ninety-one original leaves of photographs and narrative.

As you look through the pages of this volume, you will be viewing the Atlanta of 1890 through somewhat rose-colored glasses. The city that has been frozen in time by photographs is an appealing one, but the illustrations do not together present a complete portrait. The photographs were selected to represent a metropolis that had come of age, one that exhibited order, grandeur, and beauty. The pictures were individual pieces of late nineteenth-century Atlanta that symbolized a larger whole. In the case of *"The Gate City"* the sum of its parts was less than the whole of the city, for the purpose of this book was to celebrate the achievements of Atlanta, not to document all aspects of its environment. Study the photographs to see the place that is portrayed; read the text that highlights the accomplishments of an up-and-coming Southern metropolis; and fit them together into your own view of a city whose remnants can still be found today.

The Atlanta of 1890 was a place with a past and a future. Despite the protest in the introductory paragraph that this work was not intended to be historical, the opening pages of the narrative detail the early history of Atlanta. Borrowing information from E. Y. Clarke's *Illustrated History of Atlanta,* the then official history of the city, *"The Gate City"* described the 1836 Act of the Georgia General Assembly that authorized the state to construct a railroad from the Tennessee River to the southeastern bank of the Chattahoochee River where branch roads could run to Athens, Milledgeville, Forsyth, and Columbus.[1] The following year, Ste-

---

[1]E. Y. Clarke, *Illustrated History of Atlanta,* 2nd ed. (Atlanta: J. P. Harrison, [1878?]; Atlanta: Cherokee Publishing, 1971).

phen H. Long, the engineer-in-chief of the state-owned line, selected the southeastern terminus of the Western and Atlantic Railroad, the site of the future city of Atlanta and the junction from which a network of roads would spring to other cities and towns in the Southeast. The historical narrative of *"The Gate City"* continued with a list of facts from the earliest years, but, interestingly, it provided no dramatic presentation of a founding or a moment of birth for Atlanta. When Stephen H. Long drove the stake to mark the terminus of the Western and Atlantic Railroad in the fall of 1837, he was establishing the right-of-way for a transportation line, not laying out a city. But the consequence of Long's work was what E. Y. Clarke called the setting of "the foundation-stone in the marvelous superstructure of commercial prosperity today marking the spot."[2] A city did rise on the spot on which the Western and Atlantic engineer had settled, but Long himself had no responsibility in raising the child that he had helped to conceive. He left the area in 1840 after resigning his position, passing up an opportunity for half interest in a land lot of 202 acres in the heart of downtown Atlanta. He was later reported to have said that the terminus would be " 'a good location for one tavern, a blacksmith shop, a grocery store, and nothing else.' "[3]

Fifty years after Stephen Long established the site for Atlanta, President Grover Cleveland visited the city for the Piedmont Exposition. Held in the fall of 1887, the exposition was designed to celebrate the present and the future of the city rather than look to its past. Spearheaded by promoter Henry W. Grady, the 1887 exposition was intended to initiate "first-class annual fairs" that would "attract attention to Atlanta and thus be another factor in building up the city."[4] Grady, a man whose hope for the city seemed boundless, envisioned Atlanta as one of the predestined capitals of the world.[5] Although it had become the state capital after the Civil War and in 1873 had surpassed Savannah as the largest city in Georgia, Atlanta still had quite a way to go on its preordained route. Ironically, in 1887 no one thought to prepare a celebration of an important milestone along the way: the city's fiftieth anniversary. The Piedmont Exposition came and went without any attention being paid to Stephen Long's momentous choice fifty years earlier. In that same year, *Harper's Weekly* published a promotional narrative about the "Gate City" but chose to begin the city's history with the 1836 bill that authorized the construction of the Western and Atlantic Railroad.[6] Even though there was no commemorative volume in 1887, this work made three years later "to give a stranger a fairly correct idea of the city illustrated upon its pages" can serve to represent Atlanta at the age of fifty.

Atlanta in 1890, with a population of 65,533, was ranked forty-second among American cities. The railroads that had made possible urban development at this location had shaped the physical layout of the emerging metropolis. The heart of the city was Union Station, which straddled the east-west tracks dividing the town into a north and south side. Centered immediately around the station were the retail and wholesale buildings of the emerging downtown. Two- to six-story buildings were concentrated along Peachtree, Decatur, Marietta,

---

[2]Ibid., 19.

[3]Franklin M. Garrett, *Atlanta and Environs: A Chronicle of Its People and Events,* 3 vols. (New York: Lewis Historical Publishing, 1954; Athens: University of Georgia Press, 1969) 1:173.

[4]Ibid., 2:137.

[5]Mills B. Lane, *The New South Writings and Speeches of Henry W. Grady* (Savannah: Beehive Press, 1971) ix.

[6]"The Industrial South, Atlanta, Georgia," *Harper's Weekly* (12 February 1887): 111.

Whitehall, Alabama, and Broad streets. Along these congested thoroughfares, people, horse-drawn trollies, wagons, carriages, and bicycles all competed for right of way. The screeching of whistles and brakes and the smoke and steam from the locomotives were constant reminders of the nearby railroads. Farther out the tracks, to the east, west, and south, the city's factories, railroad repair shops, and supply houses could be found. Atlanta's residential neighborhoods merged into the downtown, where rich and poor, black and white could be found living. The horse-drawn and, more recently, electric trolleys had helped to establish residential avenues of distinctive houses that radiated from the downtown, but the wealthy who lived on Peachtree Street or Capitol Avenue could see houses of the working class within a block or two of their own homes.

By today's standards Atlanta in 1890 was a compact city. It was also a biracial city, divided by the color line into black and white. For the 28,000 black residents of the city (43 percent of the population), Atlanta was a mecca. Just a quarter of a century after the abolition of slavery, the city had become the location of five major institutions of higher education for blacks. Situated on high hills on the outskirts of the 1890 city, Atlanta University (whose original Stone Hall is now the Fountain Hall of Morris Brown College), Atlanta Baptist Seminary (now Morehouse College), and Spelman Seminary (now Spelman College) were located to the west; Clark College and Gammon Theological Seminary to the south (on Capitol Avenue at the present location of Carver High School); and Morris Brown College to the east (on Boulevard near the site of the present Georgia Baptist Hospital). Although black Atlantans could be found living in all areas of the city, there were three concentrations: to the east along what is now Auburn Avenue, to the west around Atlanta University, and to the south in the vicinity of what is now the Atlanta Stadium. Within these residential neighborhoods were black churches and the black grammar schools provided by the city as part of a segregated school system.[7]

The bustling, biracial city of 1890 is partially presented in this volume. For, although the photographs and narrative are intended to give "a fairly correct idea of the city," they very clearly are arranged to present Atlanta's best face. *"The Gate City"* is an early example of a genre of urban promotional literature that proliferated in American towns and cities in the last decade of the nineteenth century. This city-view book represented the convergence of several important elements of late-century urban life. First, Americans wanted visual representations to show off their growing towns and cities. A popular market for relatively inexpensive bird's-eye views had developed in the 1830s because of recent advances in the technology of lithographic printing. Among the mass of images that Americans bought to display in their homes and offices, urban views were most popular. By the 1920s, 2,400 places were represented in bird's-eye views, with thirty of the older and larger cities having had ten or more views produced in the preceding century.[8]

Bird's-eye views were prepared by a troop of traveling artists and agents who crisscrossed the United States and Canada in search of towns where there would be interest in their services. Typically the agent and viewmaker came to town to promote their project by advertising in the newspaper their intention to prepare a sketch of the city. As the agent canvassed for paid subscribers, the artist would survey the town, gathering detailed notes on street pat-

---

[7]Timothy J. Crimmins, "The Atlanta Palimpsest: Stripping Away the Layers of the Past," *Atlanta Historical Journal* 26,2-3 (Summer/Fall 1982): 13-32.

[8]John W. Reps, *Views and Viewmakers of Urban America: Lithographs of Towns and Cities in the United States and Canada, Notes on the Artists and Publishers, and a Catalog of Their Work, 1825-1925* (Columbia: University of Missouri Press, 1984) 3-4.

terns and architectural forms. Using this data, the artist would create a panoramic view from an imaginary perspective above and distant from the city, capturing all of the physical manifestations of progress. The highly stylized bird's-eye views filtered out many of the unpleasant aspects of urban life; their simplified portraits presented a town face that bore careful study. Upon close examination, cupolas and church towers could be discerned, windows and stories counted, and businesses and factories located. Prosperous urban dwellers were fascinated with these detailed renderings because they could see where they lived, worked, shopped, and worshiped. Viewmakers displayed their renditions of the cityscape to an interested citizenry who would be offered an opportunity to buy a personal copy. When there were sufficient numbers of subscribers, the agent would take the drawing to a printing house where stone or zinc etchings were prepared for a run of lithographed color prints. The agent then returned to the town to distribute the views and to sell extra copies to others looking for parlor ornaments.[9]

The mass-produced lithographic views represented a second dimension of late-century American life that helped to create a market for the new genre this volume represents—civic pride. Urban boosterism reigned supreme from fledgling interior towns to burgeoning coastal metropolises. Businessmen everywhere were looking for symbols to represent successful urban growth. What better object than a portrait that captured the city's extent, showed its principal factories and transportation facilities, highlighted its commercial blocks, illustrated its proliferation of churches and schoolhouses, and even included architectural details of some of the finer homes? While advertisements selling urban views pointed out their usefulness in demonstrating urban progress to those in distant places, these objects were most commonly used as parlor ornaments and office decorations. Merchants and businessmen who proudly hung nineteenth-century urban views were showing to their customers, clients, and out-of-town visitors that their city was a substantial place, one well worth the additional investment that would bring continued growth.[10]

In 1871 Albert Ruger, an itinerant viewmaker who produced more than 250 urban lithographs between 1866 and 1891, published a bird's-eye view of Atlanta.[11] Just seven years after the near-total destruction in the Civil War, the 1871 view represented an important milestone in the city's history. There were no scars of war in this lithograph, only signs of a prospering town. Railroad roundhouses, tracks, depots, and stations dominated the center of the view. Nearby were a dozen commercial blocks, beyond which residential structures could be seen on tree-lined streets. The list of references beneath the view included public buildings—the state house, governor's mansion, Kimball House hotel, city hall, and Union Depot; industries—planing mills, foundries, a rolling mill, iron works, grist mill, flour mill, and brewery; churches—thirteen in all; and schools—three of which were for blacks, one for whites. Just barely discernible in the far western corner of the view was a group of buildings identified as the U.S. Barracks, an oblique reminder of the recent war and the present Reconstruction.

The 1871 view of Atlanta presented the physical layout of a town with a population slightly greater than 20,000, but it also represented a hidden lesson about the city that was implicit in bird's-eye views. Nineteenth-century cities were expanding at rapid rates, constructing new buildings, growing beyond their former limits, developing industries, and forging additional transportation links. With so much that was new in the urban environment, city dwellers had

[9]Ibid., 28, 17-20, 40-41.

[10]Ibid., 61-62.

[11]Ibid., 201-203.

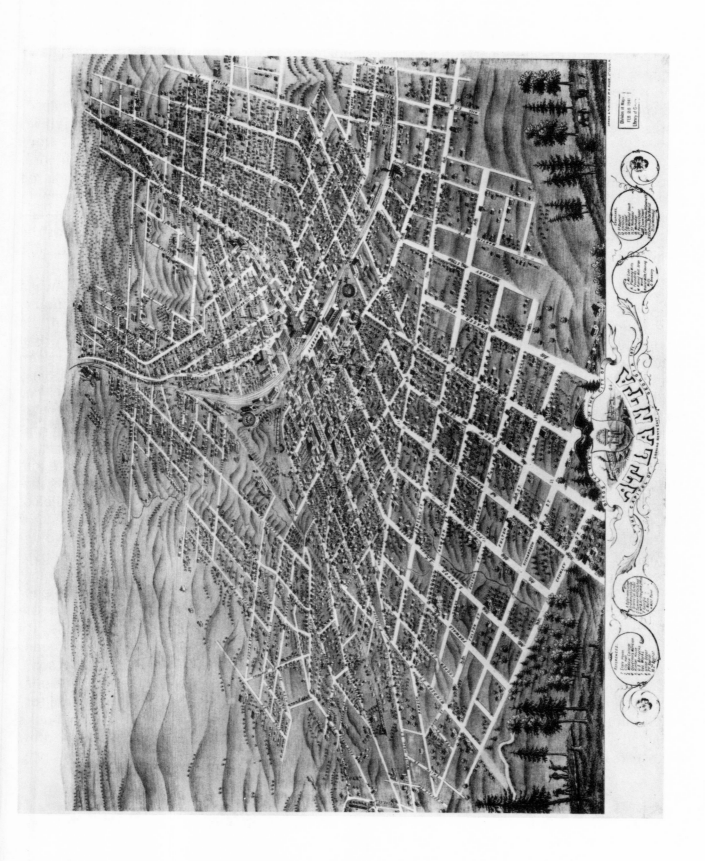

trouble comprehending both the identity and direction of these burgeoning metropolises. The bird's-eye views helped urbanites come to grips with the confusing environment in which they found themselves. First, these views enclosed the city, giving it holistic identity. Citizens could see their town with all its parts in an understandable spatial relationship. Second, the views emphasized important cultural symbols by slightly exaggerating their scale in relation to the rest of the city. In the 1871 Atlanta print the factories, railroad buildings, commercial blocks, and churches were large enough to stand out from the rest of the background. For urban promoters these structures were the symbols of progress and the signs of a prospering civilization.[12] Third, by clarifying present patterns, the views suggested the elements that were essential to future growth. In the Atlanta lithograph the prominence of roundhouses, depots, tracks, and even the tiny locomotives with their strings of freight and passenger cars pointed to the railroad as the key to the continued prosperity of the city. Good transportation connections had attracted such local industries as foundries, flour and grist mills, planing mills, and a rolling mill to process raw materials from the region. An implication of this pattern was the existence of a market for factories that processed other regional raw materials—textiles, for example.

While the 1871 bird's-eye view of Atlanta represented the prevailing medium of urban presentation and promotion for a popular audience in the latter half of the nineteenth century, *"The Gate City"* stood for a new genre whose purposes were strikingly similar to those of the lithographic views. The developing craft of photography offered novel approaches for urban promoters to show the achievements of their towns and cities and to order what appeared to many to be a chaotic environment. Photographic studies of cities proliferated in the 1890s, producing hundreds of what we would today call coffee-table books. The 1890 edition of *"The Gate City"* was followed by an imitative volume, *Art Work of Atlanta,* first published in 1895 and revised for republication in 1903. The W. H. Parrish Publishing Company of Chicago produced *Art Work of Atlanta* as one of more than sixty studies of American cities that it printed in the 1890s. The Parrish titles included cities, towns, and counties in the East, South, and Midwest, ranging in size from Portland, Maine, to Chicago. The original publisher of this volume, The Art Publishing Company of Neenah, Wisconsin, also printed photographic studies of Ashland, Kentucky, and the Valley of the St. Croix. The formula for all the books in this new genre was the same: a mixture of inexpensive, high-quality photographs with a narrative detailing the achievements and delights of a particular locale. Many of these studies were published in nine to twelve parts, giving buyers the choice of selecting among discrete sections.

The genre of city-view books was made possible by technological advances in both photography and printing. Samuel F. B. Morse introduced the earliest photographic process, the daguerreotype, to the United States in the fall of 1839 by making a picture of New York's city hall and the park that surrounded it.[13] As the century progressed, commercially produced, versatile cameras and the dry-plate process for developing pictures replaced the cumbersome and complicated techniques of daguerreotype picture making. These advances made it possible for a new generation of professionals to earn their livelihood selling images to an interested public. While these developments were taking place, a market for city-view books emerged. In 1856, G. R. Fardon produced the *San Francisco Album: Photographs of the Most Beautiful Views and Public Buildings of San Francisco,* a limited edition volume that pre-

[12]Peter Bacon Hales, *Silver Cities: The Photography of American Urbanization, 1839-1915* (Philadelphia: Temple University Press, 1984) 73.

[13]Ibid., 11.

sented individually processed photographs in a book format. Fardon produced this work in partnership with the *San Francisco Journal* for the purpose of urban promotion. Local subscribers received a personalized copy with photographs of their businesses while other books were produced for distribution to cities back in the East. The *San Francisco Album* first demonstrated a use for urban photography that would be expanded into a popular market for mass-produced books later in the century.[14]

The advances in printing technology between 1870 and 1890 provided the means to print inexpensive copies of city-view books. First came the development in the 1870s of the Woodburytype and Alberttype continuous-tone printing that, with the use of photogravure in the 1880s and the halftone process of the 1890s, made possible photographic illustration of books, magazines, and newspapers. Photogravure produced copies of photographs that had been etched on intaglio plates, while halftones were made from plates on which tiny dots created the relative lightness and darkness of a photograph. Once there was the technology to make almost limitless copies of high-quality photographs as illustrations in books, the market for city-view books dramatically expanded. *"The Gate City"* is an excellent representative of the popular city-view genre that proliferated in American cities in the 1890s.

In the 1890s both bird's-eye lithographs and city-view photography books were sold to a mass audience that was keenly interested in works that would make their cities intelligible. Atlantans could purchase *"The Gate City"* in 1890, a bird's-eye view in 1892, and *Art Work of Atlanta* in 1895. By the 1890s Atlanta businessmen were busily promoting the successes of their city. The Cotton States and International Exposition, held in Piedmont Park in 1895 as a conscious imitation of the Columbia World's Fair in Chicago two years earlier, was the most visible example of booster efforts to bring attention and business to Atlanta. The city-view books and bird's-eye view were supporting efforts in this larger strategy. The 1892 bird's-eye view was drawn by Augustus Koch, an itinerant artist who drew views for 110 towns and cities between 1868 and 1898.[15] This panorama shows considerable advancement over the 1871 view, both in artistic quality and in the growth of the city, and provides a useful comparison for *"The Gate City."*

The Koch view followed the same conventions as that of Albert Ruger in 1871: it gave a holistic picture of the city while at the same time exaggerating certain elements to emphasize progress and achievement. The most noticeable feature in the center of the 1892 print was the city's first skyscraper, the Equitable Building, an eight-story structure designed by the Chicago firm of Burnham and Root and constructed in 1891 and 1892. Dominating the expanded downtown of two dozen blocks, the Equitable Building symbolized the entry of the city into the league of leading metropolises. The new capitol was as prominent as the Equitable Building, emphasizing the prestige that this structure with classical detailing brought to the city. Railroad tracks, depots, roundhouses, and stations also stood out on the landscape, creating corridors along which were lined the smokestacks of prospering industries. A knowledgeable eye could pick out two important arrivals in the 1880s, the Exposition Cotton Mills to the northwest and Fulton Mills to the east. The key to fifty-eight sites in the city (probably selected, at least partially, through subscription) indicated an enlargement of the industrial base since 1871. Most of the industries were still involved in processing raw materials from the region; in addition to cotton, they included lumber, building materials, terra cotta, paint, and soap. Following the conventions of bird's-eye views, churches and schools were drawn slightly larger

---

[14]Ibid., 48-57.

[15]Reps, *Views and Viewmakers*, 184-86.

than scale to highlight their role in community life. So, too, the exaggerated features of Victorian houses to the north along Peachtree Street, to the south along Washington Street and Capitol Avenue, and interspersed on blocks elsewhere in the city emphasized the substantial dwellings that the business classes were erecting. One additional element could be isolated from the street grid of the 1892 city: the curvilinear drives of Grant Park, Oakland Cemetery, and the fledgling suburb of Inman Park. The landscaped park, cemetery, and suburb were important icons of late nineteenth-century urban life, which, like the Equitable Building, signaled a city having come of age.

The 1892 view presented in a format set for framing and wall display what *"The Gate City"* printed in a book designed for perusing. There was a unity to the city-view book that came in the sum of its parts rather than in the all-encompassing perspective of the bird's-eye view. *"The Gate City"* followed the conventions of other city-view books by presenting the city in its transportation lines, institutions, businesses, factories, services, social clubs, colleges, fine homes, landscaped parks, cemeteries, and suburbs. These photographs of the urban fabric represented individual contributions that together formed a united city. Their presentation in *"The Gate City"* helped Atlantans to see an order in what otherwise appeared to be a chaotic environment. They also represented important bench marks recognized by nineteenth-century city dwellers as measures of civilized life.

"The Gate City" offered in its opening pages its answer to lithographic bird's-eye views with several dramatic panoramic photographs of Atlanta, the first of "Old Atlanta" in 1864 before the burning of the city and beneath it two views of the devastation after the war (page 2). On the following page is a panorama of the downtown from what was then the tallest building in the city, the newly constructed state capitol. What more dramatic proof of urban progress than the realistic detail in photographs of the devastated town after the Civil War and contrasting perspectives of the prospering city a quarter of a century later? Panoramic views were an important type of late-century photograph because the camera could offer an alternative to the prevailing tradition of bird's-eye views. The camera offered verisimilitude in exchange for an all-encompassing map of the city. For a place the size of Atlanta, a single-shot panorama could not capture anywhere near the extent of the entire city; in its stead, the view from the dome of the capitol focused on the downtown. This was an important symbolic beginning point for the volume; it not only suggested the prosperity of the entire city, but it also set the stage for other photographs that would tell the same story. The literary convention of *"The Gate City"* was that of synecdoche, where each of the photographed parts represented the larger whole. The panorama itself presented a part of the unity that was suggested by the volume because its view included church towers, governmental clock towers, business blocks, the leading hotels, the dome of the passenger station, and the cupola of a freight depot. There were even the chimneys and roof of a simple, plantation-plain or "I" house in the bottom center of the photograph, suggesting the origins of the city described in the accompanying narrative, which detailed the construction of Atlanta's first two-story frame house (page 9). The panoramas that introduced *"The Gate City"* were more than just pictures with city buildings; they were fables to be read for a deeper level of meaning: tales of prosperity and progress, stories in which individual pieces of the city represented a much larger whole, and lessons that ordered a complex urban environment.[16]

The photographic panorama of Atlanta continued to be a staple of urban promotion in the twentieth century. Each new tower or skyscraper gave opportunities for high-angle views. *Art*

---

[16]Hales, *Silver Cities*, 73, 88.

Work of Atlanta included photographic overviews of the downtown from the Equitable Building, while promotional literature after 1906 used the Candler Building. In recent years, the skyline view has replaced the downtown panorama as the part representing the whole of the city. As more and more skyscrapers rose around Five Points and north along Peachtree Street, their profile, usually taken from the east side of the downtown, came to symbolize the achievement of Atlanta. Today the problem of using visual cues to unify the metropolis is as pressing as it was for nineteenth-century Atlantans. With skyscrapers appearing in "downtown-like" clusters in midtown, Buckhead, and along the northern perimeter highway, the central-city skyline no longer neatly represents the larger metropolis. Today the downtown skyline is a part of a part, one cluster of office towers among many in a sprawling metropolitan area.

The panoramic view from the capitol introduced the prospering downtown of 1890 Atlanta. Interspersed throughout the rest of the volume were photographs of downtown streets and buildings. The street scenes in the business district were divided into two types: those with people, wagons, and other signs of human activity and those in which people were clearly subordinated to the structures that loomed over them. The photographs on Whitehall Street (page 8), Wall Street (page 13), and Marietta Street (page 33) featured what nineteenth-century photographers called "instantaneous" views, created by fast shutter speeds that captured people moving about in the streets. By today's standards, late nineteenth-century photographs required very slow shutter speeds, so exposures for street scenes were lengthened to capture the street and buildings while emptying out people and activity.[17] Although instantaneous views could have been used more frequently, they were the exception in *"The Gate City."* It is interesting that they were used almost exclusively among the downtown street scenes in which hustle and bustle indicated the commercial vitality of Atlanta. The two photographs with the most human energy were the scene of Whitehall Street (page 8) and the view of Wall Street (page 13) where the pace of daily life competed with the buildings for the attention of the viewer.

The few bustling street scenes were important to the overall message of *"The Gate City"* for they attested to the vitality of the metropolis. There were relatively few such photographs because city-view books aimed at presenting a monumental city where the actors who found themselves caught in the turmoil of everyday life could see the orderly stage on which they performed. Buildings dominated street scenes as in the views of Wall Street and Union Depot (page 8) where the Kimball House, the depot, and the three-story buildings that framed the picture dwarfed the people in the center of the photo. In addition to the street scenes that featured numerous business buildings, many structures were singled out for individual attention, including the Chamberlin, Johnson & Co. Building (page 27), the Moore & Marsh Building (page 63), the M. C. Kiser Law Building (page 62), and the Atlanta Constitution Building (page 44). The symbolic importance of these structures justified their inclusion: two were dry goods stores, one a law office building, and one the home of a leading newspaper. While it is possible that these businesses paid to be in *"The Gate City,"* they were important nonetheless because they represented the substantial quality of commercial architecture built in Atlanta during the preceding decade.[18]

The downtown scenes and business buildings in *"The Gate City"* helped to support the central theme of the volume: Atlanta was a prosperous city. The homes of the wealthy com-

[17]Ibid., 88.

[18]Elizabeth Mack Lyon, *Atlanta Architecture: The Victorian Heritage* (Atlanta: Atlanta Historical Society, 1976) 22-36.

mercial leaders presented additional evidence. There were twenty-eight photographs of the homes and mansions of Atlanta's white elite, including a bank president (page 36), the editor-in-chief of the *Atlanta Constitution* (page 32), a real estate agent (page 73), produce merchant (page 76, top), cotton factor (page 87), and tobacco merchant (page 91). While the men who built these homes were not pictured, the substantial dimensions of the residential architecture clearly represented their achievements. In the late nineteenth century, urban boosters equated architecture with civilization; the presentation of such a wide variety of house styles in *"The Gate City"* offered proof that Atlanta stood tall by the measurement of the age. Together the handsome homes and the business buildings offered to viewers an ordered urban environment where the successful worked in prominent downtown buildings and retired in the evening to fashionable residences. Thus, while they were not introduced in person, Atlanta's entrepreneurs were the heroes of the hidden story in *"The Gate City."* The physical evidence of their activities gave sense "to an urban mythos built on that Gilded Age concept of merchant princes and their agents remaking a city to their own image."[19]

By 1890 Atlanta was more than a commercial center; it was also the location of important regional industries. So it was not just the merchant princes who were making the city in their image; industrialists also were shaping the modern metropolis. Photographs of sixteen separate factories were included in *"The Gate City"* to show the range of manufacturing. Like the industries that appeared in the 1892 bird's-eye view, these firms processed raw materials from the region or produced products for regional use. Timber from the South supplied three furniture factories, a planing mill, lumber yard, coffin factory, and piano shop, while wood by-products were used in a paint factory. Two plants manufactured gins and cotton seed machinery to process cotton, while one produced plows to prepare the soil and another fertilizer to assist the growth of the region's staple crop. *"The Gate City"* apparently intended these industries to show the diversity of enterprise in the city, rather than providing an illustration of each type. If so, it was not a major omission that the textile mills were not included.

Just as the homes of Atlanta's entrepreneurs represented the men who stood behind the commercial enterprises of the city, so the houses of local industrialists were used to spotlight this group of community builders. Two imposing structures best demonstrated this element of the taxonomy of *"The Gate City"*: the Van Winkle Gin and Machinery Company (page 38) and the residence of Edward Van Winkle on the following page. The baronial home of Edward Van Winkle attested to the prosperity of his industrial enterprise and underscored the power that this entrepreneur exerted in the community. On a more modest scale the residences of I. S. Boyd (page 89) and T. W. Baxter (page 86) suggested the more moderate success of their furniture company (page 69).

"The Gate City" presented business and industrial buildings as evidence of the economic accomplishments of Atlanta in 1890; it also provided numerous additional symbols indicating the city's membership in the class of leading American cities. While each city had its own signs of progress and achievement in the genre of city-view books, major hotels were usually selected because they "served as symbols of prosperity, civic advancement, and nostalgic cues for visitors."[20] The vantage point for these photographs was usually the street, from which the angle made the buildings appear even larger than life. Typical of this approach, the Kimball House (page 6) seemed to dwarf the people, horses, and wagons at street level. Located across Wall Street from Union Depot (page 8), the seven-story Kimball House, which had

---

[19]Hales, *Silver Cities*, 70.

[20]Hales, *Silver Cities*, 91.

been completed only five years earlier, represented the High Victorian style which became the dominant look in late nineteenth-century Atlanta architecture.[21] The massive building loomed large in the consciousness of both Atlantans and visitors. On the occasion of its opening, *Harper's Weekly* had said: "the building has a distinct suggestion of Dutch Renaissance in which the New York of two centuries ago was built; of which so many examples are to be seen in Holland and North Germany, and which is peculiarly appropriate, by its expression of quaint and comfortable domesticity, to the uses of an inn."[22] It was frequently in the news in reports of the activities of visiting dignitaries and mentioned as the place of meetings and dinners of the city's civic leaders. When President Grover Cleveland and his recent bride came to visit the 1887 Exposition, they shared its bridal chamber.[23] Hotels continued to be important icons in Atlanta. Three-quarters of a century after the publication of *"The Gate City,"* another hotel came to symbolize the promise of Atlanta: in the late 1960s the Regency Hyatt House was used to represent the progressive dynamism that distinguished the city from its counterparts elsewhere in the South. In the most recent decade the Peachtree Plaza Hotel has dominated the downtown skyline just as the Kimball House did a century earlier.

Of equal symbolic importance in *"The Gate City"* was the state capitol (page 71). The photograph, which was taken from the tower of Central Presbyterian Church across Washington Street, emphasized the monumental nature of this classically inspired structure. The five men who were posed on the steps in the center of the picture were sufficiently small to emphasize the building's mass. If *Harper's Weekly* could relate the style of the Kimball House to structures in Holland and North Germany, contemporary observers surely would have noted parallels between the capitol and the great works of Greece and Rome. Here again, the photograph presented a portrait of an Atlanta icon, a sign of permanence and stability, a foundation from which a prosperous future would arise.

Another important element of the iconography of city-view books was the landscaped park. Americans in the nineteenth century had witnessed remarkable transformations in their environment; not only had more people begun to live in cities, but the size of cities had dramatically increased. From the 1860s on, efforts to bring order to rapidly expanding urban areas had included the provision of public open spaces in the form of urban parks and parkways. Parks provided a picturesque landscape that gave dramatic relief from the congestion of much of the urban environment. But contemporaries saw parks as more than just refuges from the burgeoning city; they believed that they would help to civilize urbanites. "The public park was one of those rare institutions embodying the spirit of a society: its utopian goals, specific social needs, and form of expression."[24] Some argued that parks could serve as the centers of a new community life; others wanted them to serve as necessary places of relief for the poor who were crowded in tenements; and most believed that recreation in these open spaces was an uplifting antidote to antisocial behavior.[25] It was no accident, then, that the opening photograph in *"The Gate City"* was a view in Grant Park.

---

[21]Elizabeth M. Lyon, "Change and Continuity: Atlanta's Historic Business Buildings," in *The American Institute of Architects Guide to Atlanta* (Atlanta: American Institute of Architects, 1975) 28.

[22]Garrett, *Atlanta and Environs* 2:60.

[23]Ibid., 150.

[24]Albert Fein, *Frederick Law Olmsted and the American Environmental Tradition* (New York: George Braziller, 1972) 9.

[25]Ibid.

Five photographs (pages 1, 5, 18, 41) and three pages of text (pages 30, 34, 37) were devoted to Grant Park. Frederick Law Olmsted had championed the cause of urban parks, beginning with his design of New York City's Central Park in 1858. By the 1880s his landscape principles were used throughout the United States. *"The Gate City"* reported that after Lemuel P. Grant had donated his land for development as a park, Charles Boeckh, an accomplished civil engineer, created a topographical map, and Major Sidney Root acted as superintendent overseeing the construction of the grounds. It was a testament to Atlanta that such a picturesque setting could be created in so short a time. In 1885 Mayor George Hillyer noted,

> The L. P. Grant Park becomes more and more a source of pride and satisfaction to our citizens. The amount apportioned to its improvements in the past year was small, being only three thousand dollars, but it has been economically and well expended. . . . A place of recreation like this is of inestimable value to our hard-working and industrious population. Nothing promotes more, both the moral and mental, as well as physical health, than such a place of resort and recreation.[26]

Mayor Hillyer echoed the arguments offered by nineteenth-century park proponents: Grant Park would promote the moral, mental, and physical health of an industrious citizenry. By 1890, *"The Gate City"* demonstrated that Atlanta had created a park whose natural beauty was "equaled only by Druid Hill Park in Baltimore" (page 30).

The presentation of Grant Park in *"The Gate City"* follows the conventions of nineteenth-century urban photography, which presented the park as

> (1) a refuge from the denaturing effects of the urban-industrial world; (2) an extension of the monumental and orderly grandeur of renaissance-induced rebuilding and a set-piece for the symbols of urban civilization; and (3) a locale for Victorian pleasure seeking in exotic natural surroundings.[27]

The photographs in this volume presented Grant Park as a refuge. The two scenes of Lake Abana (pages 1, 5) showed representative Atlantans who were enjoying the solace on "a very charming sheet of water" with picturesque qualities amplified by the text.

> In the centre of the lake is a small island, built securely of rock and sand, and blooming richly in summer with blossoms of bright color. A small willow dips its slender fingers downward from the middle of the mound and adds a pretty effect to the scene. (page 34)

Lake Abana was depicted as a place where Atlantans could go to contemplate the beauties of nature, away from the hustle and bustle of urban life. The scene of the avenue (page 41) reinforced the idea that one could escape from the pressures of the city by driving down the road that disappeared into a stand of trees. The photograph beckoned the viewer to escape into the woods, while the text described "lovely drives through the park along shady roads and blossoming hills" (page 30).

"The Gate City" presented Grant Park as a refuge in nature, but it also linked the park to the new urban form of 1890 Atlanta. There were numerous views of residential avenues with a perspective that was similar to that of the avenue in Grant Park (page 41); in these, the eye of the viewer was drawn along tree-lined streets on which were located the houses

---

[26]Garrett, *Atlanta and Environs* 2:41.

[27]Hales, *Silver Cities*, 104.

of prosperous Atlantans. The views of Peachtree Street (pages 7, 10, 68) depicted an environment in which nature seemed to be integrated into the city. If the photograph of the Grant Park drive beckoned the viewer to the refuge of nature, the tree-lined perspectives of Peachtree Street revealed the location of homes where Atlantans could retreat from the cares of business activity. Both the leafy residential streets of the city and the idyllic paths in the park were part of the ideal urban form of late-century American life. In this arrangement, the downtown was the place of commerce, the transportation corridor was the location of industry, and the outlying suburbs and parks the places where respite was taken from the world of work. Herein lay the order that Americans imposed on the rapidly expanding urban environment of late nineteenth-century America. The photography and text of *"The Gate City"* presented Atlanta in this ordered way to its readers.

Urban parks were also places for Victorian pleasure-seeking in exotic natural surroundings. Grant Park offered the distractions of both art and nature to those who strolled along its paths. The photograph of Bethesda Spring (page 41) revealed this double combination. There was a sentimental statue of an angel, who was, according to the text, blessing the water, which was "cold and clear and beautiful" (page 34). Across from the spring was the Tarn, "a dark looking little pool fringed with reeds and rushes, and holding a tiny island in the centre, upon which is waving a tall caladium and clusters of ferns and cat-tails." There were four other springs in the park, as well as art for contemplation. The statuary included two bronze lions (page 18), an eleven-foot-high bronze stag, and "the handsomest sun dial in the world." In addition, there were "three handsomely-constructed bridges of brick and stone that are ornamented with bronze and terra-cotta vases, and four pretty rustic bridges that are quite picturesque" (page 34). The allure that the text of *"The Gate City"* promised for those who visited Grant Park was typical of the treats that landscaped parks held in store for Victorian pleasure-seekers.

"The Gate City" presented an ordered portrait of Atlanta in which the park had a particular place in the form of a changing city. Equally important to the symbolic arrangement of the nineteenth-century city were two closely related urban pieces, the suburb and the cemetery. The 1892 bird's-eye view revealed both of these elements in the Atlanta landscape. Of the two, the suburb was the more important. Frederick Law Olmsted also championed the planned suburb as a necessary way to tame the wild tendencies in urban growth. In Olmsted's view, "Public parks were meant to be a countervailing force in the essentially commercial city, improving the urban environment; the planned suburb was a part of the city in the countryside. All of the care taken to design the public park according to the social needs of the users and the physical demands of a given site was now to be applied to the planned community."[28] There were many photographs in *"The Gate City"* of suburban-like scenes, but Inman Park, the city's first planned suburb, was still an embryo in 1890. The brief essentials were provided in the text.

[Inman Park] is a most delightful residence portion of Atlanta. . . . A number of handsome residences have already been built and new ones are in process of construction. A picturesque park has been laid out and enclosed. . . . In this park are groves, springs and a beautiful little lake which is shown in the views in this work. It is certainly a most charming portion of the city, and an ideal spot for a home. (page 85)

[28]Fein, *Frederick Law Olmsted,* 32-33.

The three photographs of Springvale Park (pages 11 [number 5], 15) in the center of the developing Inman Park revealed how a community was planned for the social needs of its users. The view at the top of page 15 pictured a house in the background of the romantic scene. The Grant Park views showed similar picturesque arrangements intended for a public who had to travel there for relatively short visits. In Inman Park, families could live in immediate proximity to the landscaped park, partake of its fruits, and still participate in the civilizing influence of the nearby city with its schools, libraries, churches, and other social institutions. The link to the city was apparent in the photograph at the bottom of page 15: in the upper right-hand corner stood the electric trolleys that carried husbands to work and wives and children to shop and socialize downtown. While the urban park offered temporary refuge from the pressures of commercial competition, the suburb provided a more lasting escape. Each evening the breadwinner could retreat to this country-like environment to reconstitute himself for the next day. Meanwhile, his spouse and children were sheltered from the noise and congestion of the city.

The photographs of three Inman Park houses (pages 84, 90, 91) indicated that this planned suburb was still in the early stages of development. Two of the homes (pages 84, 90) had no owner listed; they stood waiting for those who would find the suburb "a most charming portion of the city, and an ideal spot for a home" (page 85). *"The Gate City"* presented a more finished look to another outlying residential community, West End. Four photographs (pages 24, 28, 32) depicted substantial homes and a view of a park. The park was actually part of the estate of Evan P. Howell, whose house could be seen on page 32 and in the left center of the park view on the bottom of page 24. While *"The Gate City"* had no text describing the suburban town that had grown up three miles southwest of Atlanta, the *Atlanta Constitution* provided a portrait of the suburban refuge in 1890.

> West End is emphatically a residence community. There are no manufactories with soot and dust, no paupers, but a thrifty, well-to-do class of people, who generally own their homes, who have their garden, their flower yards, their horse and cow and fowls, and, who, away from the noise and dust and strife of the great city, live in quiet and comfort.[29]

Trolleys had opened West End for development in the 1880s, just as the electric motor line on Edgewood made Inman Park accessible in the 1890s. The trolley that served West End also traveled on to another essential element of an ordered city in the nineteenth century, West View Cemetery.

Rural cemeteries, burying grounds in park-like settings, had been established as adjuncts of growing cities in the 1830s: Boston's Mount Auburn in 1831, Philadelphia's Laurel Hill in 1836, and New York City's Greenwood Cemetery in 1838. Designed with picturesque landscaping and sentimental statuary so that both nature and art would capture the attention of visitors, rural cemeteries predated urban parks as places of recreation. Atlanta's Oakland Cemetery began as a burying ground, but, as the 1892 bird's-eye view suggested, it had come to resemble in appearance its grander cousins in cities of the Northeast.[30] *"The Gate City,"* noting that city officials had prohibited further burials in Oakland for sanitary reasons, devoted its attention to West View Cemetery with two views (page 42) and a paragraph of text (page 52). Located just beyond West End, West View was designed on the newly fashionable

---

[29]*Atlanta Constitution,* 27 April 1890.

[30]Dana F. White, "Landscaped Atlanta: The Romantic Tradition in Cemetery, Park, and Suburban Development," *Atlanta Historical Journal* 26, 2-3 (Summer/Fall 1982): 99-102.

"landscape lawn plan" rather than the forested arrangement of the rural form. Having opened four-and-a-half years earlier, by 1890 the 582-acre cemetery (four times the size of Grant Park) had five-and-a-half miles of drives over a countryside of grassy lawns. Statuary had been erected to memorialize some of the 2,650 interred there, while more than 10,000 ornamental trees and shrubs had been planted to punctuate the terrain (pages 42, 52).

The order that *"The Gate City"* imposed on the burgeoning city in 1890 could be seen in its presentation of the landscaped triad: Grant Park, Inman Park, and West View Cemetery. Along with fashionable homes on tree-lined streets, these features were defining the outlying extent of the metropolis. To the south, the city had constructed a Victorian pleasure garden; to the west, a private land company had carved out a lawn cemetery; and to the east, another developer was constructing a park-like suburb. In between these large-scale developments, the fashionably adorned fingers of the city's streets reached out to shape a similar environment. The scenes along Washington, West Peachtree, and Peachtree streets and in West End presented a picture of the calm, carefree life to be found in picturesque refuges on the fringe of the nineteenth-century city.

While the 1892 bird's-eye view presented easily discernible urban districts, *"The Gate City"* provided images of small pieces of the city that the viewer had to organize into a coherent whole. The subject matter and the angle of view in the photographs were the cues that pointed to the order underlying the seeming chaos of late-century city life. The shots of store-lined streets and commercial buildings were unified as the downtown depicted in the opening panorama; the photographs of railroad tracks and factories blended into an industrial district near the heart of the city; and the pictures of landscaped streets linked together the parks, suburbs, and cemetery in the outlying areas of Atlanta. In addition, *"The Gate City"* offered a neatly divided arrangement of the cultural life of the city by featuring buildings of prominent religious, educational, and social institutions.

Churches occupied a prominent place in the physical environment of 1890 Atlanta as well as in the affairs of daily life. The towers of several churches stood above the city in the panorama from the capitol (page 3); most noticeable were Central Presbyterian and the Shrine of the Immaculate Conception. Five churches—one Baptist, two Methodist, and two Presbyterian—were featured together in "Atlanta Views" (page 60). Saint Philip's Episcopal (page 62) had a page all to itself, while the interior of the Congregational Church of the Redeemer was featured with a half-page photograph (page 53). The pictures of these buildings followed the conventions of late-century architectural photography: the street-level perspectives (pages 60, 62) emphasized the monumental character of these community institutions. The buildings themselves were signs of prospering congregations and, by extension, a thriving city. Their inclusion in *"The Gate City"* was representative. They indicated that there was a religious dimension to life in Atlanta, even though structures of each denomination were not pictured. As in other city-view books, the churches were an essential part representing the larger whole of the city.

Educational buildings were given extended coverage in *"The Gate City"* because they demonstrated that Atlanta had become a regional center for secondary and collegiate instruction. These schools represented the architectural achievements of the preceding decade; they exhibited a wide variety of Victorian styles in structures of substantial size. The photographs of the "Technological School" (page 49), Atlanta University (page 51), and Spelman (page 75) were taken at a distance from the buildings with trees and shrubbery occupying the foreground. This perspective, along with the campus scenes at Gammon Theological Seminary (page 54) and Clark University (page 55), visually tied the school buildings to the suburban and park views interspersed throughout the book. As a result, the educational institutions were presented as refuges, places where students could escape the pressures of city life to pursue learning. The narrative emphasized the suburban character of the schools. Clark University's "magnificent campus comprising almost 500 acres . . . [lay] just outside of the limits of the city of Atlanta," with trolley cars leaving "the corner of South Pryor and Alabama streets every twenty minutes" (page 74). Spelman had grounds "extensive for recreation," with "delightful walks in every direction." It, too, was linked to Atlanta by streetcar lines. Of Gammon Theological Seminary, the text noted, "A more central, accessible, healthful and beautiful site cannot be found in all the South" (page 85). There was a clear booster message in the presentation of educational institutions in *"The Gate City"*: because of its excellent location, Atlanta had been chosen for the important role of regional education center. With its convenient trolley system, the city provided direct connections between its thriving downtown and the picturesque campuses in its outlying suburbs. At the conclusion of the section on Spelman Seminary, *"The Gate City"* spelled out its booster theme: "Atlanta has been chosen as the location of the school, because its healthful climate, railroad connections, and spirit of enterprise, have made it largely the political, commercial and educational centre of the state" (page 65).

The portraits of school buildings in *"The Gate City"* offered another, more subtle, message to its readers: Atlanta was taking steps to deal with race, a major challenge facing cities in the South. Of the six educational institutions that were spotlighted, five served black students. There was hardly an overt mention of race, only the one description of Atlanta University, whose students were drawn "from the colored population of adjacent states, as well as from all Georgia" (page 74). For those who wanted to know about the 42 percent of the population that was black, the schools provided the lesson. They were being educated by a curriculum that prepared them for their stations in life. The narrative detailed the programs of instruction at Atlanta University and Clark University, which included industrial training for boys, domestic economy for girls, and academic preparation for future teachers (of black children in the South). The account of the program at Clark pointed to a "thorough college course," with a standard of scholarship "as high as at any school in the South," but the implied message was that black children were being educated for positions within a segregated society.

"The Gate City" narrative for Atlanta University erroneously implied state support for the institution. In listing the sources of financial support, it noted that "For several years an annual appropriation of $8,000 was made by the state" (page 74). The implication from this statement was that Georgia was funding advanced education for both blacks and whites, at separate institutions. The only problem was that Georgia had withdrawn its public subsidy of Atlanta University because children of the white faculty attended. In the 1880s the administrators and most of the faculty at Atlanta's black colleges were white. At Atlanta University, white teachers saw nothing wrong with having their children educated with their black pupils. Interpreting this as a challenge to the separation of the races, the Georgia General Assembly withdrew its annual payment of $8,000.[31] Of course, *"The Gate City,"* because of the booster nature of the publication, did not mention this. The surface portrait of Atlanta was that of a city dealing positively with race. This had been the final message of Henry W. Grady, who shortly before his death in December 1889 had addressed the Boston Merchant's Association. There Grady summarized the view of race held by late-century white Atlantans, a perspective that is implied in *"The Gate City."*

---

[31]Clarence A. Bacote, *The Story of Atlanta University: A Century of Service, 1865-1965* (Princeton: Princeton University Press, 1969) 88-101.

Meantime we treat the negro [sic] fairly, measuring to him justice in the fulness the strong should give to the weak, and leading him in the steadfast ways of citizenship that he may no longer be the prey of the unscrupulous and the sport of the thoughtless. We open to him every capacity. We seek to hold his confidence and friendship, and to pin him to the soil with ownership, that he may catch in the fire of his own hearthstone that sense of responsibility the shiftless can never know.[32]

A portrait of a prosperous city would not have been complete without some treatment of its social institutions. *"The Gate City"* represented this aspect of Atlanta life with photographs from the Capital City Club, the Y.M.C.A., and the Elks. The Capital City Club House (page 7) was located on Peachtree Street in a block of fine homes that included the governor's mansion. Founded in the preceding decade, the club symbolized the existence in the city of a large, prosperous merchant and industrial class. The photograph of the clubhouse tied the structure visually to the mansions of the elite along Peachtree Street. The Y.M.C.A., on the other hand, was more democratic; its middle-class membership numbered 500 (page 26). The exterior view (page 45) depicted a Richardsonian-Romanesque business building in the downtown, while the interior photographs (pages 46 and 47) showed the parlor and reading room where the uplifting activities of the organization took place. The Y.M.C.A. extended the promotional message of *"The Gate City"* because it was "without doubt one of the finest Y.M.C.A. buildings in the country" (page 26).

"The Gate City" was shaped by a variety of editorial decisions that influenced its form as well as that of other city-view books. It was, first and foremost, part of a promotional genre. The introduction to the *"The Gate City"* noted that its "illustrations have been selected with reference to what would give the best variety of features" (page 1). In other words, the photographs were selected to present the best face of Atlanta in 1890. There were no scenes of poverty, no shots of bedraggled children, no indication of the pervasiveness of the color line. To have found these dimensions of urban life, readers would have to purchase another book published in 1890, Jacob Riis's *How the Other Half Lives,* the influential account that used photography to document the problem of poverty in New York City. Riis's exposé and *"The Gate City"* represented two divergent styles of late nineteenth-century urban photography. The former showed how cities were failing to provide a humane environment to a significant portion of their people, while the latter demonstrated the order that underlay the burgeoning metropolis, and, in the process, celebrated its achievements.[33]

Jacob Riis was a self-trained photographer because he could not interest a professional in his subject matter. By the late nineteenth century, specialization among photographers had resulted in much stylistic homogeneity. Some photographers earned a livelihood making stock studio portraits, while others went out into the streets at the behest of clients. From this latter group came architectural photographers, who by the 1890s had become handmaidens to architects, their task being one of fading into the background of their pictures so that the newly constructed building would be spotlighted. While Riis could not persuade any professional from this group to travel with him in the slums of New York, publishers of city-

---

[32]Edna H. L. Turpin, *The New South and Other Addresses by Henry Woodfin Grady* (New York: Haskell House Publishers, 1904, 1969) 117.

[33]Hale, *Silver Cities,* 163-64.

view books employed them to capture the beauty in the late nineteenth-century urban environment.[34]

The stylistic conventions of architectural photography were apparent in *"The Gate City."* There was a similarity in the techniques of composition between draftsmen who rendered line drawings of how a proposed structure would appear and architectural photographers who documented the appearances of a building after construction was completed. While these illustrations seemed to be realistic renderings of buildings, they were actually arranged to show off the structures, permitting their use as a promotional tool by the designer. Both line drawings and photographs were used to highlight the work of architects in *"The Gate City."* The renditions of the Hill Building (page 31, number 4) and the Law Building (page 62) best illustrated how unacknowledged artists created prints that celebrated the work of named architects. Both the photograph of the Hill Building and the line drawing of the Law Building were made from the same perspective: the structures were framed in the center of the illustrations where architectural details stood out and where the buildings appeared to dominate the street and surrounding stores. The intention of these pictures was to show the artistry of the architect rather than the virtuosity of the photographer or draftsman. The goal of architectural photography was transparency; it was to be a medium through which the art of building form could be viewed.

Transparency was a key element in all the photography in *"The Gate City."* Of the illustrations in the volume, only the view of the capitol had the photographer identified. This anonymity in *"The Gate City"* helped to explain the artistry of the volume. Its illustrations were to be windows through which Atlanta could be viewed, rather than vehicles exhibiting the particular style of a photographer. If the volume was a work of art, the artistry lay in the city it presented: the architectural qualities of its business buildings, homes, schools, churches, and clubs; the monumentality of its hotel and capitol; and the picturesque elements of its suburbs, parks, and cemetery. Photography was the medium for the presentation of the city, where the angle of vision captured the best side of the subject.

The introduction of *"The Gate City"* claimed that the volume would be "a fair delineation of the city of Atlanta," but the promotional purposes behind its publication clearly influenced both the kind of photography that was used and the subject matter of the illustrations. By using the literary convention of synecdoche, this city-view book presented individual photographs of streets, buildings, and landscape to represent larger urban patterns. The portrait of Atlanta in this volume was partial, one in which "the city became a place of monumental scale and inexorable progress, where laissez-faire capitalism was successfully converting urban entropy into a new civilization—an environment of order, grandeur, and permanence."[35] The Atlanta that was presented was fascinating nonetheless; it captured the achievements of a city barely fifty years old and it preserved for future generations what has indeed become of historic interest.

---

[34]Ibid., 175-77.

[35]Ibid., 119.

" THE GATE CITY."

ATLANTA

HISTORICAL,

DESCRIPTIVE AND PICTURESQUE.

1890:

ART PUBLISHING COMPANY,

NEENAH, WIS.

VIEW IN GRANT PARK.

THE CITY OF ATLANTA.

━━━◆━━━

THIS publication is not intended to be an historical work. The design is to furnish in a work of art, a fair delineation of the city of Atlanta. The illustrations
have been selected with reference to what would give the best variety of features, and also
with a view of preserving for the future what might become of historic interest. The
passing years bring change to everything over which they take their flight, and whatever may be the destiny of this city it will be interesting in after years to look upon
the features of former years. Again, this work is widely circulated, and it is intended
to give a stranger a fairly correct idea of the city illustrated upon its pages. As the
various pages are turned, there passes before the eye the various characteristics of the
city. The following historical and descriptive matter is gathered and compiled from
authentic sources, and is condensed into a few statements of the more important facts.

Atlanta is known as the Gate City of the South, and in view of its location the
designation seems eminently appropriate. The city lies just a little east of an air
line drawn from New York, and exactly on one drawn from Richmond, Va., to New

OLD ATLANTA, 1864.

TAKEN FROM ELLIS STREET, BETWEEN COLLINS AND CALHOUN, KNOWN THEN AS "COLLEGE HILL," NOW CLIFFORD STREET.

2

BIRD'S-EYE, FROM DOME OF CAPITOL.

Orleans, and is very near midway between the last named cities. From the Atlantic cotton belt ports it is only distant about 260 miles, and from the Mexican Gulf ports 270, and from the Mississippi about 340 miles. The Gate City is specially favored as to centrality, altitude, and temperature—1050 feet above sea level—with a mean temperature of 42 degrees in winter and 76.9 degrees in summer, and with a central location between the consuming marts, the South Atlantic coast and the Gulf of Mexico. The climate of Atlanta is unsurpassed, being remarkably mild and equable —a medium between that of the tropical and cold temperate latitudes. Since the foundation of the city, the difference between the coldest and hottest summers has ranged between 86 degrees and 92 degrees, and that between the coldest and mildest winters from 60 degrees to 8 degrees; the mercury in thermometers rarely falling within 10 degrees of zero, and indicating an annual mean of 64 degrees Fahrenheit. It is never uncomfortably warm here; the nights are always cool and breezy. The greatest heat is, on an average, considerably less than that which prevails contemporaneously in New York, Philadelphia, Cleveland, Detroit, Chicago and other Northern cities, the warm weather, however, continuing for a much longer period than in the cities named. The altitude of Atlanta, and the dryness and purity of the air, so mitigate the heat that one scarcely realizes the range of the mercury, and labor is done in the streets, upon buildings and other exposed places, in safety at a temperature which would be fatal in the North.

The healthfulness of Atlanta is proverbial. In fact this part of the State is eminently salubrious, presenting, as it does, a favorable exhibit of all the features essential to health, such as elevation, drainage, dryness of air, and exemption from epidemic and malarial visitations. Situated so high on porous soil, which drinks the rain in, and thereby prevents humidity of the atmosphere, and the noxious influence consequent upon the decomposition of vegetable and animal matter; removed far from miasmatic generation of stagnant marshes and ponds, with a vegetation unproductive of matter inimical to health, and possessing an abundance of pure water, distributed in pipes throughout the city, Atlanta is comparatively free from zymotic diseases, and absolutely so from those of a malignant or epidemic character.

EARLY HISTORY.

The first house on the site of Atlanta was a log shanty, built by Hardy Ivy in 1835. His nearest neighbors were at Decatur, and for three years no other building encroached upon his domain.

Georgia was one of the first states in the Union to recognize the importance of steam transportation, and in 1833 the Legislature chartered the Central, Georgia and Monroe railways. In 1835 an act was passed authorizing the "construction of a railroad from the Tennessee line, near the Tennessee river, to the southwestern bank of the Chattahoochee river, at a point most eligible for the running of branch roads

VIEW IN GRANT PARK.

THE H. J. KIMBALL HOUSE.

L. B. WHEELER, ARCHITECT.

VIEW ON PEACHTREE STREET.

CAPITAL CITY CLUB HOUSE.

VIEW ON WHITEHALL STREET.

WALL STREET AND UNION DEPOT.

thence to Athens, Madison, Milledgeville, Forsyth and Columbus." The peculiar requirements of the act made it necessary for Stephen H. Long, the engineer-in-chief, to establish the eastern terminus of the road not at the Chattahoochee, but seven miles east of it, near the present passenger depot. The selection of this point was the most fortunate that could have been made—it was at the intersection of three great mountain ridges, along which a few years later were constructed the Georgia Central, and Atlanta and West Point railroads. The State road gradually progressed, and in 1842 the first engine for it was brought in a wagon all the way from Madison. It was a great event, and people came for twenty miles to see it.

In 1839 Mr. John Thrasher arrived here and built the second house, and also put up a building for a store. The firm of Johnson & Thrasher carried on the store, being the first business firm in the place. The place was first called "Terminus," on account of its being the terminus of the railroad. Willis Carlisle, in 1842, opened a store near the First Presbyterian church on Marietta street. His daughter was the first white child born in the community. She married Mr. Walter S. Withers.

About this time the first two-story frame house was built. It was on the square on Pryor street, opposite the Kimball house, and was first used as an office by the State road authorities. Along in the early forties, before there was any railway communication with the outside world, the good people of Terminus and vicinity lived in primitive fashion. Most of the houses were mere log cabins, and some of them had dirt floors. The wants of the people were very simple. They carried the products of their farms to the stores and bartered them for dry goods and groceries. There was a regular and considerable wagon traffic kept up with Augusta, and there were professional wagoners who made it their business to haul cotton and grain and the skins of wild animals down to Augusta, where they exchanged their freight for all kinds of goods to be carried back to the dwellers in the wilderness. In 1843 there were seven families here. Just beyond where the Governor's mansion now stands was the burying ground. In December, 1843, an act of the legislature made Terminus a name of the past. The little village was incorporated under the name of Marthasville, in honor of the daughter of Governor Wilson Lumpkin. In 1844 Mr. Jonathan Norcross started a saw-mill—the first factory. Other stores were opened, and Marthasville saw a boom in prospect. The follwing year the first newspaper, the Luminary, was started under the editorial conduct of the Rev. Joseph Baker. It was a small weekly, and its subscription list was slim, but it did a good work for Marthasville. During this year the Georgia railroad was completed, and the first train came through, with Judge John P. King, the president of the road, and a big party of notables. George W. Adair was along, being the first conductor to make the trip. A small building for church and school purposes was erected in 1845 on Peachtree street, near the present First Methodist church. Dr. J. S. Wilson probably preached the first sermon in it, and in 1847 a union Sabbath school was organized in it.

According to Clark's "History of Atlanta," there were only about a dozen families in 1845, perhaps one hundred persons in all. Among these was Stephen

MONUMENT OF THE LATE BENJ. H. HILL—CORNER OF PEACHTREE AND
WEST PEACHTREE STREETS.

RESIDENCE OF EDWARD C. PETERS—PONCE DE LEON, CIRCLE.

10

1—CONFEDERATE MONUMENT, OAKLAND CEMETERY.

2—CORNER OF PEACHTREE STREET AND PONCE DE LEON CIRCLE.

3—GOVERNOR'S MANSION.

4—VIEW ON PEACHTREE STREET.

5—INMAN PARK.

11

Terry, dealer in real estate; James A. Collins, merchant; Dr. George G. Smith; A. B. Forsyth, grocer; Joseph Thomason, W. Crawford and Harrison Bryant, workmen; Jonathan Norcross, merchant; J. Thrasher, who had returned from Griffin; William Kile and the Ivy family. There were two general stores, one kept by Collins & Loyd, and the other by A. B. Forsyth, for whom E. A. Werner clerked. Kile had a small grocery, and Dunn had a bonnet and hat store. On the southwest corner of Marietta and Peachtree was the storehouse of Jonathan Norcross, and in it was to be found S. B. Hoyt, who was the clerk. In 1846 the Macon & Western, or Central railroad, was finished, and the event was celebrated by a big mass meeting, at which Daniel Floyd, Mark A. Cooper and others made speeches. More newspapers were started. The Democrat, by Dr. W. H. Fernerdon; the Enterprise, by Royal & Yarborough, and the Southern Miscellany, by C. R. Hanleiter. The following year the population had reached three hundred. The Baptists began building a church. I. O. and P. E. McDaniel erected the first block of brick stores, the other brick buildings being the Atlanta Hotel and the railroad depots. Two Masonic lodges were chartered.

In 1846 Mr. J. Edgar Thompson, chief engineer of the Georgia railroad, in a letter to Richard Peters, also an engineer of the road, suggested "Atlanta" as a good name for the growing town. He derived it from the word "Atlantic." The name caught the popular fancy; it was in everybody's mouth, and when a new charter for a city was obtained the next year, Atlanta became the legal name. The charter was drawn by J. Norcross, John Collier and J. Vaughn. In 1848 the first city election was held, and Moses W. Formwalt was elected mayor, with Jonas S. Smith, B. F. Bomar, R. W. Ballard, James A. Collins, A. W. Walton and L. C. Simpson council- men. After this everything went ahead with a rush. Wesley chapel, the First Bap- tist, the First Presbyterian, St. Philip's and a Catholic church were built. Z. A. Rice, J. Norcross, I. O. McDaniel and B. F. Bomar started the Intelligencer, which paper afterward grew into a daily. Kay & Ramsey started the Daily Examiner.

The State road was completed in December, 1849.

The first fire was on Alabama street in 1850.

First regular bank was started in 1850, with $300,000 capital, by George Smith of Chicago.

First fire company organized in 1851.

Large flouring mill built by Richard Peters in 1851.

Winship foundry started in 1851.

The first lawyer was L. C. Simpson.

Atlanta & West Point railroad finished in 1852.

The first daily paper by Kay & Ramsey, started in 1853, called "The Examiner."

City hall built in 1854.

City lit by gas in 1855.

First military company, the "Gate City Guards," organized in 1857.

Young Men's Christian Association organized in 1857.

First directory published in 1859.

VIEW FROM MARIETTA STREET.

VIEW ON WALL STREET.

13

RESIDENCE OF W. A. HEMPHILL—PEACHTREE STREET.

RESIDENCE OF CLARENCE KNOWLES—PONCE DE LEON, CIRCLE.

14

INMAN PARK.

INMAN PARK.

15

BANK INTERIOR OF AMERICAN TRUST AND BANKING CO.—ATLANTA, GEORGIA.

16

The name "Gate City" was first applied to Atlanta at a banquet given at Charleston in 1856. In a toast to Atlanta the term "Gate City" was used, and the title has attached to the city ever since.

In 1859 a sketch written for the City Directory contained the following items: Among other things the sketch said that the city's population in 1854 was 6,025. After that year it increased about 1,000 per annum, and in 1859 it was 11,500 souls.

The assessed value of real estate was $2,760,000.

The number of stores, exclusive of saloons, was 57, and the amount of goods, sold in 1858 was about $3,000,000. There were four hotels, four large machine shops, two planing mills and sash and blind factories, three or four tanneries, one or two shoe factories, a rolling mill turning out thirty tons a day of railroad iron, and clothing factories employing seventy-five hands.

In 1861 the population was 13,000.
Atlanta was under martial law in 1864, and the population was 20,000.
Battles of Atlanta July 20 and 22, 1864.
Atlanta captured by Sherman September 2, 1864.
Entire population exiled from the city September 12, 1864.
City destroyed—some six hundred houses, November 16, 1864.
Citizens began to return December, 1864.
City limits enlarged to three miles diameter in 1866.
Young Men's Library started in 1867.
The "Constitution" newspaper started in 1868.
DeGive's opera house and Kimball house built 1870.
Union passenger depot built 1871.
First street railroad September, 1871.
The public school system opened January, 1872.
New charter of Atlanta, February, 1874.

ATLANTA REBUILT.

We find the following account of the work of rebuilding after the close of the war: The first steps towards the rebuilding of Atlanta after the surrender at Appomattox were made under great difficulties. People rushed in from every direction. Mr. V. T. Barnwell, whose Directory has already been mentioned, says that the city during the year 1865 presented quite a picturesque appearance. Small houses built of the remnants of other buildings were put up for rent. Mayor Calhoun was re-elected, and was succeeded the following year by Hon. James E. Williams. During the last six months of 1865 the council licensed about 338 business firms, representing various branches of trade. Very little manufacturing was done. Hoge, Mills & Co. started a planing mill on Marietta street. The railroads rebuilt their depots and shops; the market houses were built; the corporate limits were extended so as to

VIEW AT FORT WALKER IN GRANT PARK.

HEBREW ORPHAN ASYLUM.

GEO. L. NORMAN, ARCHITECT.

RESIDENCE OF HOKE SMITH, ATTORNEY AT LAW AND PRESIDENT OF THE ATLANTA JOURNAL.

WORKS OF THE ATLANTA BRIDGE AND AXLE COMPANY, ATLANTA, GA.

inclose an area of a circle three miles in diameter; John D. Gray & Co. started the Atlanta rolling mill on Marietta street; brick business blocks were erected; street railroads were introduced, and at the end of 1866 the assessed value of real estate was $7,000,000, and the amount of goods sold in a year was estimated at $4,500,000. The population was shown by a city census to be 20,228 souls. Most of the old citizens returned after the war, and with them came an influx of settlers from the Carolinas, Tennessee, Kentucky, Virginia and the Northern states. In 1870 Atlanta was the second city in the state in population, standing next to Savannah. Three years later she stood first, having 30,869 inhabitants, and in 1890 the population is probably 75,000. The reconstruction of the state and the election of a republican administration in 1867 caused the capital to be changed from Milledgeville to Atlanta. This change was heartily indorsed by a democratic majority in 1877, and the new million dollar state house just completed shows that the capitol is here to stay.

Almost as soon as a settled government was re-established, the enterprise of our people began to manifest itself in a thousand ways. Splendid stores and churches, and a handsome opera house were built. The Kimball house sprang into existence, and after its destruction by fire in 1882, it was rebuilt on a grander scale. The Air-Line railway was completed in 1873, and gave the city a new impetus, the results of which may be seen in the other railroad enterprises which will be found properly set forth in the chapter devoted to them. Atlanta began years ago to attract attention as a "convention city." State fairs were held here, and the great International Cotton Exposition in 1881, matched by the Piedmont Exposition of 1887, drew crowds from all parts of the country. Not a year passes without national gatherings here of some great body, the Locomotive Brotherhoods, the Engineers, the firemen, a commercial convention, a Y. M. C. A. reunion, the Prison Reform Association or something equally notable.

POPULATION.

The population of the city of Atlanta at different periods is given in the following table:

1855	.	.	6,025	1875	.	.	30,869
1861	.	.	13,000	1880	.	.	37,409
1864	.	.	20,000	1883	.	.	49,517
1865	.	.	10,000	1885	.	.	56,837
1870	.	.	21,788	1890	estimated,		75,000

THE Y. M. C. A.

In this work will be found an excellent representation of the Young Men's Christian Association building. For a number of years the work was done in rented rooms, but at a meeting of the International convention here in 1885 the happy

RESIDENCES OF H. H. CABANISS AND E. P. BLACK—PEACHTREE STREET.

VIEW ON PEACHTREE STREET.

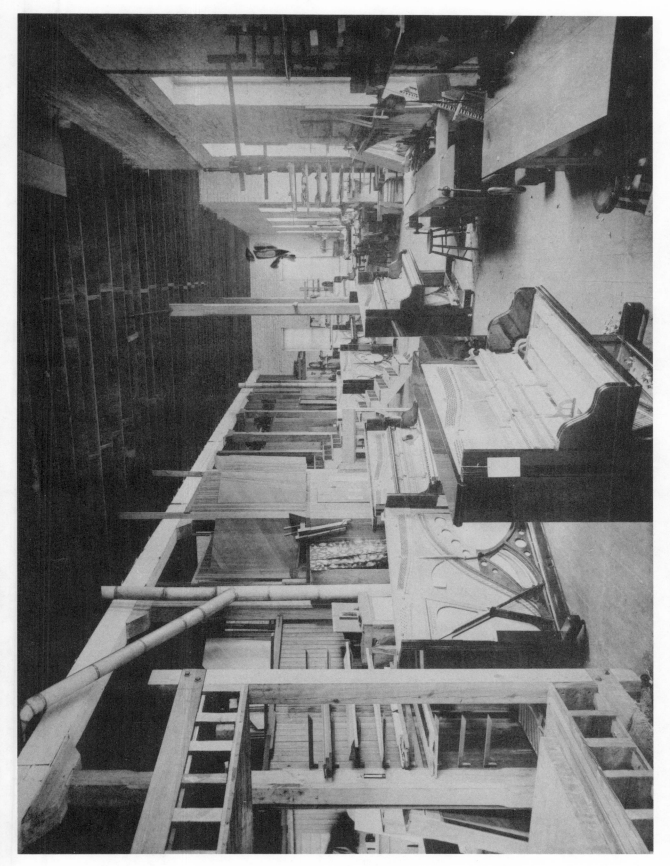

ATLANTA PIANO MANUFACTURING COMPANY—FINISHING AND REGULATING ROOM.

RESIDENCE OF CLARK HOWELL, JR.—WEST END.

VIEW AT WEST END.

24

INTERIOR OF STATE LIBRARY.

thought was conceived of erecting a suitable building in which the meetings could be held and the work in hand be properly accomplished. To this end a voluntary subscription list was opened in the city with such immediately flattering results that the building was begun the following year, 1886. The building stands at the corner of Pryor and Wheat streets, and is without doubt one of the finest Y. M. C. A. buildings in the country. The association was organized before the war, but its records were lost and the association broken up. In 1873 it was reorganized, and at present has a membership of at least five hundred. The cost of the building furnished was about $100,000.

RAILROADS.

One of the chief factors in Atlanta's present prosperity is, undoubtedly, her excellent railroad facilities. Eight great lines center here. They are the Central, the Georgia, the Richmond & Danville (Piedmont Air Line), the Atlanta & West Point and Western Railway of Alabama, the Atlanta & Florida, the Georgia Pacific, the Western & Atlantic, and the East Tennessee, Virginia & Georgia. In addition to these there are now the following roads either projected or in course of construction: Georgia, Carolina & Northern, the Atlanta, Atlantic & Western, and the Marietta & North Georgia. No city in the Union surpasses Atlanta in the completeness of her transportation facilities.

THE CHAMBER OF COMMERCE.

Some time during 1866 the merchants of Atlanta organized a Board of Trade. About a score of the most sagacious and enterprising—among them R. M. Clarke, Glenn, Wright & Carr, Bell, Moore & Co., Zimmerman & Verdery, Pratte, Edwards & Co., A. K. Seago, W. R. Phillips & Co., Henderson, Chisholm & Co., R. M. McPherson, W. M. & R. J. Lowry, W. J. Garrett, A. C. & B. F. Wyly, Langston & Crane and J. R. Wylie—met in Mr. R. M. Clarke's office, then on Whitehall street, and organized by electing Mr. Clarke, president, J. S. Peterson, secretary, and Perino Brown, treasurer. J. W. Clarke, the president, was soon succeeded by Hon. W. M. Lowry, who continued to hold the office until 1871, when he resigned. Appreciating the importance of the institution and believing that the time had come for a reorganization on a firmer basis, a general convention of business men was held in July, 1871, and the following month the name was changed to the Atlanta Chamber of Commerce, the officers being Major Benjamin E. Crane, president, and M. E. Cooper, secretary. In May, 1883, a meeting of merchants and citizens was held for the purpose of devising means for extending the usefulness of the organization. It was decided to provide more commodious quarters for the association, and the result was the erection of the present Chamber of Commerce building. Work was begun in November, 1883, and the building completed the following year. The officers the present year, ending July, 1890, are: J. G. Oglesby, president; Paul Romare, treasurer; H. G. Saunders, secretary.

CHAMBERLIN, JOHNSON & CO. BUILDING.

W. H. Parkins, Architect.

27

RESIDENCE OF GEO. F. BOLLES—WEST END.

28

LAKE LAMONT AT LITTLE SWITZERLAND.

VIEW AT LITTLE SWITZERLAND.

ATLANTA PARKS.

There are some delightful spots in and around Atlanta, and a stranger would be surprised to find so many features common to the most famous summer resorts. The L. P. Grant park is the most noted and extensive of the pleasure resorts. This beautiful park originated in the gift to Atlanta early in 1883 of 100 acres of land on the southeast edge of the city by Col. Lemuel P. Grant. In the spring of 1888 the city purchased forty-five on the north edge of the park, so that there are now 145 acres. It is a lovely spot, admirably adapted to the purposes for which it was donated. The park is not only attractive on account of its natural beauty, which is said to be equaled only by Druid Hill park in Baltimore, but is interesting as a historical spot, there being two lines of fortifications running throughout the entire length of the grounds. At the highest point in the park is Fort Walker, where stands a pedestal of Hallowell granite, upon which will be mounted in the near future a stone statue of Peace, which will be ten feet high. This fort was reconstructed exactly on the original line, and shows one of the most splendid views of Atlanta to be had from any other point around the city. Four brass cannon, which are a loan from the state, are mounted here, and two valuable bronze lions, which cost $500, guard the entrance to the spot. Gen. William H. T. Walker was killed in the battle of Atlanta on the 22d of July, 1864, about a mile and a half from the fort, and in his memory the place is named.

Next in point of interest is McPherson walk, named for General McPherson, who was killed upon the same day as was General Walker, between Atlanta and Decatur, in the woods lying east of the fort. Thus do these two points bring to mind the hero of the blue and the gray, who fell each for his country's aid. In May, 1883, an accurate topographical map was made of the park by Mr. Charles Bœckh, who is an accomplished civil engineer. Since then many improvements have been made in the park, and many interesting features added. In the same year Major Sidney Root was appointed president, superintendent, etc., and has continued to hold the position to the entire satisfaction of every one in the city.

There are lovely drives through the park along shady roads and blossoming hills, and these are named after the principal cities and towns in Georgia. The principal drive is Savannah avenue, the name being given to it because of its being the longest in the park, and because of Savannah being the oldest city in the state. The length of the avenue is one mile and a half, and circles the entire space that is covered by the grounds of the park. Next in length is Americus avenue, which is over a half mile in length, and then Augusta, one-half mile long; Macon, a quarter of a mile; Brunswick, one-quarter; Columbus, one-quarter, and Rome, one-quarter—Milledgeville being only one-eighth of a mile long.

The springs are numerous and are all delightfully situated at the foot of some lovely sloping hill, or by the side of some beautiful walk, over which the boughs of the overhanging trees sway and swing in the breeze. The water of all the springs,

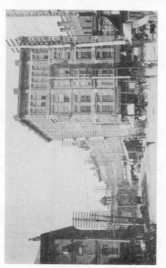

1—VIEW ON PRYOR STREET.

2—ARLINGTON HEIGHTS—REMAINS OF EARTHWORKS USED IN SIEGE OF ATLANTA. 3—INMAN PARK.

4—THE HILL BUILDING, (G. C. NORMAN, ARCHITECT.)

5—BROAD, FROM MARRIETTA STREET. 6—CORNER OF WASHINGTON AND MITCHELL STREETS.

RESIDENCE OF EVAN P. HOWELL—WEST END.

RESIDENCE OF W. W. BOYD, FORSYTH STREET.

VIEW ON MARIETTA STREET.

save one, is freestone and it is cold and clear and beautiful, one being sulphur and iron principally. Their names are Bethesda, Saloam, Constitution, one without a name, and the Sulphur Spring. Over Bethesda, which is at the foot of a lovely ivy-grown hill, stands a large statue of an angel, blessing the water, a gift of Major Root. Opposite this charmingly situated spring is the "Tarn," a dark looking little pool fringed with reeds and rushes, and holding a tiny island in the centre, upon which is waving a tall caladium and clusters of ferns and cat-tails. This is one of the prettiest parts of the park, and the shade is dense and pleasant on the hottest day. Frogs croak hoarsely in the water as they bask lazily in the reeds and blink stupidly in the sun, and the songs of the birds and the rustling of the leaves make a sweet music in the air. The walks are: Emerald, which winds down beside the branch, Germania, McPherson and Serpentine. Near the latter is a tall bronze stag, eleven feet high, which cost the park commissioners nearly four hundred dollars.

Lake Abana is a very charming sheet of water and is supplied from the various springs around the park, the water being conducted to it by under-ground pipes. To the south of the lake is a tall, wooded hill from which comes a fragrant breeze perfumed with resinous pine and wild flowers, and which slopes gradually to the grass fringe of the blue-crinkled waters. On the lake there are eleven boats, each bearing the name of a flower, and these are used constantly by visitors who pay a nominal sum for the privilege of rowing on the water. In the centre of the lake is a small island, built securely of rock and sand, and blooming richly in summer with blossoms of bright color. A small willow dips its slender fingers downward from the middle of the mound and adds a pretty effect to the scene. The boat house, boats and refreshment stand are rented out by the year, and last year the net profits of the boats alone was fifteen hundred dollars. By the side of the lake there is a stand where horses and carriages can be protected alike from the sun and rain.

Beyond the lake is a magnolia lawn which makes a brilliant patch of color in the park, with its beds of scarlet salvia, dusty miller, colias, gentian bloomers and ageratum, which blend in a harmony of blue and red and silver. The centre bed on this lawn is laid off in the form of an opened magnolia, but on account of the many trees of that variety the lawn is named. Around the lawn is the bicycle track, which is a quarter of a mile long and which is said to be one of the finest in the South. This lies in the northwest corner of the park and at the far end of the lake. There is now in progress a lawn-tennis and croquet ground, and this will be a very attract-ive addition to the new part of the park, and will be situated near the big pavilion. There are three handsomely-constructed bridges of brick and stone that are orna-mented with bronze and terra-cotta vases, and four pretty rustic bridges that are quite picturesque. All these add a charm to the scene and make the park much more at-tractive in appearance.

It is said that the handsomest sun dial in the world is out at the park. It was the gift of Mr. W. F. Herring, and stands conspicuous on Savannah avenue. It is

ATLANTA PIANO MANUFACTURING CO.

LABORATORY OF SWIFT'S SPECIFIC COMPANY.

RESIDENCE OF T. B. NEAL, WASHINGTON, STREET.

made of bronze, and is thirty-three inches in diameter. The work is from the hand of the eminent optician, H. Waldstine, of Union Square, N. Y., who exercised the greatest care and skill in his labor, and took three months to complete the work. The dial shows Atlanta's sun time. The face is elaborately engraved by hand, and upon the outer and larger plate are indicated fifty of the world's principal cities, showing their air-line distances in statute miles from Atlanta. Jerusalem is 6,439 miles; Melbourne is 9,679 S. E.; Pekin, 7,171 W. by N. W.; Buenos Ayres, 5,611, nearly S.; Nanking, 7,641, nearly W.; Constantinople, 5,756, E. by N. E.; Berlin, 4,767, N. E.; Sacramento City, 2,076, N. W.; and St. Petersburg, 4,981, N. by N. E. The dial plate alone cost $1,000, and the dial is mounted upon a granite pedestal nearly three feet high.

There are two large and handsome pavilions in the park, a music stand, a boat house, two refreshment stands and other less important buildings, which are used for various purposes.

The Zoo, which has but recently been added to the park through the kind donation of Mr. George V. Gress, has added much to the interest already felt in this resort, and it consists of: 1 Hyena, 2 Silver lions, 1 Black bear, 1 Jaguar, 1 Elk, 2 Fawns, 2 African lionesses, 3 Monkeys, 2 Wild cats, 1 Coon, 1 Mexican hog, 1 Camel, 1 Dromedary. Mr. Gress could not have manifested his great interest in the welfare of Atlanta, in any way that would be more appreciated than in this liberal gift which contributes so much to one of the most interesting features of the city.

Peters' Park is owned by a private corporation. It is located on West Peachtree street and North avenue. It contains 200 acres, is undulating and covered with oaks, and has been quite prettily improved.

Ponce de Leon Springs. These two springs, one freestone and the other mineral, have gained a wide-spread reputation for the medicinal qualities of the water. They are situated just outside the northeastern limits of the city.

Angier Springs. Another mineral water spring located just south of Ponce de Leon Springs. This spring also has well established medicinal properties.

Little Switzerland adjoins Grant park, and is a delightful resort. The grounds are beautifully and tastefully laid out; flowers, trees and shrubs are in profusion. Cool streams flow through the garden and end in a charming little lake, on which are to be found good pleasure boats.

OTHER OBJECTS OF INTEREST.

The Artesian Well is located at junction of Peachtree and Marietta streets. The drilling was commenced in September, 1884, and completed October, 1885. A depth of 2,044 feet was reached. The water supply is obtained from a depth of 1,160 feet, and the yield is 12,000 gallons per hour. The tower is eighty-five feet high, built of wrought iron and steel.

WORKS OF THE VAN WINKLE GIN & MACHINERY COMPANY.

RESIDENCE OF E. VAN WINKLE, WEST PEACHTREE STREET.

PAINT AND VARNISH WORKS OF F. J. COOLEDGE & BROS., ATLANTA, GA.

On Line of W. & A. R. R., E. T. Va. & Ga. R. R.

40

AVENUE IN GRANT PARK.

BETHESDA SPRING IN GRANT PARK.

41

IN WEST VIEW CEMETERY—BATTLE OF EZRA CHURCH FOUGHT HERE, JULY 28, 1864.

IN WEST VIEW CEMETERY—BATTLE OF EZRA CHURCH, WAS FOUGHT HERE.

Fort McPherson, U. S. A. Post is situated at the western end of the city, beyond limits. Construction was authorized by act of congress, March 3, 1885. Site was selected by the late Major General Hancock the following May. Ground was broken July, 1886, and the Post will probably be completed in 1892, at an estimated cost of $500,000. Capacity at present is four companies and band. When completed the capacity will be a regiment of ten companies. The reservation has an area of 236 3-5 acres and eighteen brick buildings are already completed, consisting of officer's quarters, double barrack, triple barrack, hospital, guard house, stable, etc. The sewer and water system is complete, and fine macadamized roads traverse the entire reservation. The garrison will consist of headquarters, staff, band, and four companies of the Fourth Artillery.

The Hill Monument is a beautiful base of marble capped by a life-sized statue of the late Benjamin Harvey Hill, in whose memory the monument was erected by his fellow-citizens. It occupies a commanding position at the junction of Peachtree and West Peachtree streets.

The McPherson Monument was erected by the Army of the Cumberland to the memory of General J. B. McPherson, and stands on the spot where that gallant Federal soldier fell on July 22, 1864. The monument consists of a massive granite pedestal and a piece of heavy ordnance, with suitable inscription. The monument is enclosed by a railing composed of the barrels of muskets. It stands in the native forest about a mile and a half beyond the southwestern limits of the city, and within a few hundred yards of "McPherson Avenue," which can be reached by following the Flat Shoals road.

Oglethorpe Park lies just outside the northwestern limits and adjacent to Mairetta street. The great "International Cotton Exposition" was held here in 1881. The buildings are now used as a cotton factory.

Piedmont Exposition Association have built spacious exposition buildings, and improved and beautified the grounds. The unparalleled success of the last fair has induced the association to hold one this year, and in every succeeding October an exposition can be expected. An adjunct of the Piedmont is the Gentlemen's Driving club. The two associations have recently consolidated, and now own in common a tract of 200 acres near the northeastern limits. It can be reached by cars on Peachtree street, the Air Line railroad or drive *via* Boulevard.

ATLANTA CEMETERIES.

Atlanta has two beautiful cemeteries.

Oakland Cemetery is situated one mile east of the centre of the city. It contains about eighty-five acres, beautifully laid out and kept scrupulously neat. It lies between the Georgia railroad and Fair street, just west of the Fulton cotton mills,

ATLANTA CONSTITUTION BUILDING.

44

ATLANTA Y. M. C. A. BUILDING.

PARLOR IN Y. M. C. A. BUILDING.

46

Y. M. C. A. READING ROOM.

47

RESIDENCE OF JULIUS L. BROWN, WASHINGTON STREET.

48

TECHNOLOGICAL SCHOOL.
Bruce & Morgan, Architects.

VIEW ON HUNNICUTT AVENUE.

49

ALABAMA STREET.

51

ATLANTA UNIVERSITY.

and is reached by either the Decatur Street cars or Fair Street dummy. It belongs to the city, whose officials have recently prohibited its further use as a burying ground on account of sanitary reasons. A very large space has been set aside as the last resting place of the known and unknown who gave up their lives for the Confederacy. A large granite monument marks the spot. It is generally conceded that no cemetery in the South surpasses Oakland in beauty.

Westview Cemetery consists of 582 acres, owned by the Westview Cemetery association. It is run on the landscape lawn plan, and the company guarantees perpetual care to the entire grounds. It is located southwest of the city, and about three miles from the centre; is reached by drive out Gordon street (W. E.) through West End; by the West Mitchell Street road, and by the old Barracks road; also by a dummy line starting from junction of Broad and Marietta streets. The grounds are said, by competent engineers, to be the finest for cemetery purposes in the country. A receiving tomb, with a capacity for 108 bodies has been built, 5 1-2 miles of drives opened up, 4 1-2 miles of sewers laid, over 10,000 ornamental trees and shrubs set out, and 2,650 interments have taken place since the grounds were opened some four and a half years ago. In this cemetery also is reserved a space for the bodies of Confederate veterans. This spot is historical, and is a portion of the line of fortifications where the battle of July 22, 1864, was fought.

THE STATE CAPITOL.

When General James Oglethorpe founded the Colony of Georgia in 1733 on Yamacraw Bluff, now Savannah, that place was the capital and continued to be until 1780, when it was removed to Augusta. In 1782 it was moved back to Savannah. The first legislature of Georgia met in a brick house on Broad street in Savannah on January 7, 1755. In 1795 Louisville, Ga., was made the seat of government and continued such until 1804, when Milledgeville was selected. The building was completed in 1812, and cost $300,000. As early as 1847 a movement was begun to locate the seat of government in Atlanta. In 1853 the people voted almost overwhelmingly for "no removal," 30,000 voting for Atlanta. In 1859 Milledgeville again carried the day. In 1867 the Constitutional convention assembled in Atlanta. The constitution was amended by making Atlanta the seat of government and providing for the building of a new capitol.

In 1870 the city of Atlanta donated $130,000 of city bonds for the purchase of a capitol, the disposition of which was set forth in a letter from Mayor Ezzard as follows: "To be used in the purchase by the state of the building now used as a state capitol; the property when so purchased to become absolutely the property of the state; also to donate any unoccupied ten acres of land within the corporate limits that may be selected by the general assembly to be used for capitol purposes.

INTERIOR OF CHURCH OF THE REDEEMER—CONGREGATIONAL.

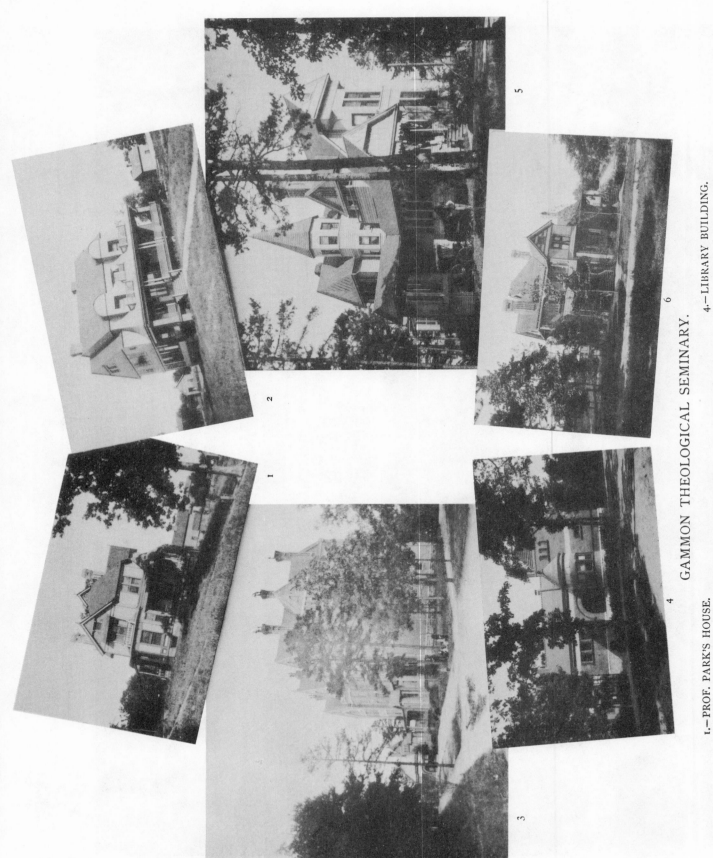

GAMMON THEOLOGICAL SEMINARY.

1.—PROF. PARK'S HOUSE.
2.—PROF. CRAWFORD'S HOUSE.
3.—GAMMON HALL.

4.—LIBRARY BUILDING.
5.—PRES. THIRKIELD'S HOUSE.
6.—PROF. MURRAY'S HOUSE.

CLARK UNIVERSITY.

1.—LOOKING TOWARD WARREN HALL.
2.—WARREN HALL.
3.—THE MODEL HOME.

4.—PRESIDENT HICKMAN'S HOUSE.
5.—TRADE SCHOOLS.
6.—CHRISMAN HALL.

PLANT OF THE ATLANTA GAS LIGHT COMPANY.

PLANT OF THE GATE CITY GAS LIGHT COMPANY.

RESIDENCE OF E. P. CHAMBERLAIN, WHITEHALL STREET.

GREENHOUSES OF EDWARD WACHENDORFF—ATLANTA.

Also to furnish free of cost to the state a mansion suitable for His Excellency, the governor of this state, for the term of ten years from June 1, 1868." The H. I. Kimball opera house was bought for the use of the state at a cost of $380,000. In 1877 the people of the state ratified the location of the capital at Atlanta by 99,149 for location to 55,201 against it.

In 1880–1, Hon. Pope Barrow introduced a bill for the erection of a new capitol, but it failed to pass. At the next session the bill by Hon. Frank Rice appropriating $1,000,000 for the erection of the new capitol, was passed. This magnificent structure was completed in the winter of 1889. The capitol is so situated that it may be seen from any part of the city and from the suburbs, and itself commands a view, from its windows and dome, of probably twenty miles of the surrounding country. A view of the structure is given in this work.

The State Library room is also shown in this work and is one of the most beautiful sections of the new capitol, and is also a magnificent reception room. The librarian, Colonel John Milledge, is one of the most efficient officers in the employ of the state, and the present excellent system which prevails in that department is due to him. It seems quite appropriate that the grandson of Georgia's governor, after whom the former capital was named, should preside over the department preserving the printed laws and records from colonial days to the present. As well known in the state, Colonel Milledge is very soldierly in bearing and tastes, and has been commissioned lieutenant colonel of the First battalion of Georgia cavalry. There are some rare relics in the library room belonging to Colonel Milledge, which are of great interest. One is a clock at least one hundred and fifty years old, which has always been kept in Colonel Milledge's family, and to-day ticks away the minutes as regularly as it did a century and a half ago. Hanging upon the wall are several commissions issued to ancestors of Colonel Milledge two hundred years ago.

The "executive mansion" in Atlanta was once the grandest house in the city. It was built by Mr. John H. James as a residence, and was afterwards bought by the state for more than $100,000. It is a large, roomy, comfortable house, unpretentious, though handsome and substantial. A beautiful grove in front comes up to the very steps, giving the house a retired appearance, almost rural.

ATLANTA BAPTIST SEMINARY.

The Atlanta Baptist seminary, under the name of The Augusta Institute, was founded at Augusta, Georgia, in May, 1867. It was conducted under the auspices of the National Theological institute, by Rev. J. W. Parker, D. D. No permanent location having been secured for it thus early in its history, it was taught at night in Springfield Baptist church. When Dr. Parker had been in charge but three months, feeble health compelled him temporarily to suspend his labors and return North. During his absence, at his request, Rev. J. Mason Rice took the principalship, and continued it until the following fall when Dr. Parker returned to his post of duty.

PARLORS OF THE ATLANTA LODGE, No. 163, B. P. O. ELKS.

ATLANTA VIEWS.

1.—FIRST BAPTIST CHURCH.   2.—WASHINGTON STREET, OPPOSITE THE CAPITOL.
3.—FIRST METHODIST CHURCH, SOUTH.   5.—TRINITY METHODIST CHURCH, SOUTH.
4.—VIEW ON MARIETTA STREET.

FERTILIZER WORKS OF GEO. W. SCOTT MANUFACTURING CO.—ATLANTA, GA.

LAW BUILDING OF M. C. KISER.

BRUCE & MORGAN, ARCHITECTS.

ST. PHILIP'S EPISCOPAL CHURCH.

MOORE & MARSH BUILDING.

WINSHIP MACHINE COMPANY.

THE ATLANTA LUMBER COMPANY.

In the fall of 1879 the seminary was removed to Atlanta, Georgia, and given its present name, The Atlanta Baptist seminary. An eligible lot of four acres was purchased, and a commodious brick building was erected for its use at the corner of Elliott and West Hunter streets. Subsequently a lot of fourteen acres was purchased and a comfortable brick building, four stories high, was erected. The institution is doing an excellent work.

SPELMAN SEMINARY.

This school was opened in the basement of Friendship Baptist church, April 11, 1881, by the present principals. There the work of instruction was carried on for nearly two years. The school was opened with eleven pupils. The aggregate number during the eight years has been over 4,130, and the present property, which is valued at over $85,000, consists of several acres of land, four double houses, described on page 4, Rockefeller hall, and Packard hall.

These buildings are situated on one of the most elevated, quiet and lovely spots within the limits of the city, and afford superior facilities for acquiring a thorough education, with economy in expenditure and preservation of morals. In point of healthfulness the location is unsurpassed. Rooms are large, airy, well heated and ventilated, and neatly furnished. Grounds are extensive for recreation, and there are delightful walks in every direction. Access is easy by two street car lines,—Broad street and Whitehall street; the former leaves the corner of Marietta, and passes very near the seminary.

Atlanta has been chosen as the location of the school, because its healthful climate, railroad connections, and spirit of enterprise, have made it largely the political, commercial and educational centre of the state.

ATLANTA UNIVERSITY, ATLANTA, GA.

This institution was incorporated in 1867, and opened in 1869. It has 650 students, under twenty-eight officers and teachers, in all grades of study from the Primary school up through grammar, normal and collegiate courses. It gives industrial training to its boys in wood-working, iron-working, mechanical drawing and farming; and to its girls in cooking, sewing, dressmaking and domestic economy. It was founded by the American Missionary association, but is now under an independent board of trustees. Its first president was Rev. Edmund A. Ware, who died in 1885. Its present president is Rev. Horace Bumstead, D. D. Its religious training is thoroughly Christian but strictly unsectarian. Its more than 200 graduates from the normal and college courses are spreading their leavening influence throughout Georgia and surrounding states. More than two-thirds are teaching, a number of them being principally of city schools. Hundreds of under-graduates are also teaching every year.

ATLANTA FURNITURE MANUFACTURING COMPANY'S WORKS.

CORNER BROAD AND WEST HUNTER STREETS.

66

RICHMOND AND DANVILLE RAILROAD SHOPS.

THE SOUTHERN AGRICULTURAL WORKS.

67

VIEW ON WEST PEACHTREE STREET.

VIEW AT EAST TENNESSEE, VIRGINIA AND GEORGIA RAILROAD SHOPS.

THE "BOYD & BAXTER FURNITURE FACTORY."

McPHERSON MONUMENT.
Spot Where GEN. JAMES B. McPHERSON was Killed, July 22, 1864.

GREEN HOUSES OF F. H. GLAZIER.

70

GEORGIA STATE CAPITOL.

From Photograph by Kuhn.

ATLANTA FIRE DEPARTMENT.

RESIDENCE OF W. M. SCOTT, WASHINGTON STREET.

CORNER ALABAMA AND PRYOR STREETS.

Its finest building, Stone Hall, which is used for chapel, recitation and lecture rooms, library, laboratory and offices, is the gift of the late Mrs. Valeria G. Stone of Malden, Mass. The Knowles Industrial building is a memorial of the late L. J. Knowles Worcester, Mass.

Current expenses are met about one-third by payments of students, the remainder by benevolent contributions including appropriations from the American Missionary association and state's fund. For several years an annual appropriation of $8,000 was made by the state. Students are drawn to this institution from the colored population of adjacent states, as well as from all Georgia by the high reputation it has earned by its strict discipline and thorough course of study.

CLARK UNIVERSITY

Established in 1868 has from a small beginning risen to the position of one of the most successful, most thorough and best-equipped schools in the South. The magnificent campus comprising almost 500 acres lies just outside of the limits of the city of Atlanta at the head of Capitol avenue. The buildings are new and commodious.

Instruction is given in the various departments of learning from the common branches to a thorough college course. Upon an adjoining campus stands Gammon Theological seminary offering advantages to those who are preparing for the ministry. The standard of scholarship at Clark university is as high as at any school in the South.

A school of domestic economy for young ladies is maintained in conjunction with the other work of the university by the Women's Home Missionary society.

A thorough normal department offers unsurpassed advantages to those students who desire to fit themselves for teaching.

Music is made a prominent feature in the work of the school.

The industrial department maintains a blacksmith shop, wheelwright shop, carpenter shop, paint shop, harness shop, foundry and printing office, beside a class in mechanical drafting. The shops are in charge of skillful mechanics, and we guarantee to turn out as good work and as fine finish as can be done in the South. Some of the best wagons, carriages, harness in Atlanta, were made here. Printing unsurpassed for neatness. Foundry, blacksmith and carpentry work promptly attended to. Rates the very lowest.

Cars for Clark university leave the corner of South Pryor and Alabama streets every twenty minutes.

GAMMON THEOLOGICAL SEMINARY.

Faculty: Rev. Wilbur P. Thirkield, D. D., president, and professor of practical theology; Rev. James C. Murray, B. D., professor of exegetical theology; Rev. Edward L. Parks, D. D., professor of systematic theology and instructor in elocution; Rev. William H. Crawford, B. D., professor of historical theology; Prof. William H.

SPELMAN UNIVERSITY—ROCKEFELLER AND PACKARD HALLS.

ATLANTA BAPTIST SEMINARY.

RESIDENCE OF J. J. FALVEY, HILL STREET.

RESIDENCE OF JAMES D. COLLINS.

PHŒNIX PLANING MILL.

GATE CITY COFFIN FACTORY.

ATLANTA PIANO MANUFACTURING COMPANY, FINISHING AND REGULATING ROOM.

RESIDENCE OF HON. FRANK P. RICE.

RESIDENCE OF MRS. JOSEPHINE RICHARDS.

RESIDENCE OF W. W. GOODRICH.

FRANKLIN PUBLISHING COMPANY.
CORNER WEST ALABAMA AND FORSYTH STREETS.

BEAUTIFUL TYROL—No. 24 PONCE DE LEON AVENUE.
JULIUS HARTMAN, PROPRIETOR.

RESIDENCE OF GEO. W. HARRISON.

FENLEY FURNITURE COMPANY.

MANNING FURNITURE COMPANY.

RESIDENCE AT INMAN PARK.

Crawford, librarian. The seminary is located at the head of Capitol avenue, one-half mile south of the city limits of Atlanta, Georgia. The campus contains thirty acres of rolling land. Steam street cars run to its edge, and its buildings overlook the city. A more central, accessible, healthful and beautiful site can not be found in all the South. The campus contains Gammon hall, the new library building, four commodious and beautiful houses for professors' families, and eight comfortable cottages for married students.

Gammon hall is a handsome building of fine modern architectural design. It was erected and furnished at a cost of $30,000. It is built of brick, with stone trimmings, and is one hundred and ten by fifty-two feet and four stories high. The students' rooms are large and well ventilated, and each floor is provided with baths.

The new library building is one of the most convenient and beautiful structures of its kind in the South. Its dimensions are sixty-eight by forty-eight feet. Its foundations are of granite, with cut-stone trimmings. The super-structure is of brick, trimmed with heavy rock-faced stone and terra cotta, with tasteful romanesque ornamentations. Students have free access to the theological library of 7,500 volumes, consisting of works in all departments of theology and related branches. It is classified and arranged by departments, in alcoves, for convenient reference with a full card-catalogue

The seminary is under the general control of the Freedmen's Aid and Southern Education society of the Methodist Episcopal church, exercised through a special board of trustees. It is in the broadest sense denominational—not sectarian—and cordially welcomes ministers and candidates of all evangelical denominations to the full privileges of the institution. The fact that during the past year there were seventy-six students in attendance representing thirteen states, more than a score of institutions of learning and five denominations, is a testimony to the wide influence and catholic spirit of this central theological seminary of the South.

Dr. Atticus G. Haygood says: " It is to be questioned whether any single institution under the care of the Methodist Episcopal church holds a place of importance and responsibility equal to that which is possible to the Gammon Theological seminary. . . . It may well be questioned whether any single institution in the Southern states could not be better spared."

INMAN PARK.

This is a most delightful residence portion of Atlanta. Edgewood avenue, a broad and beautiful thoroughfare connects this section with the central portion of the city. This suburb is the property of the East Atlanta Land company, as is also the electric motor line which is operated on Edgewood avenue. A number of handsome residences have already been built and new ones are in process of construction. A picturesque park has been laid out and enclosed by the company. In this park are groves, springs and a beautiful little lake which is shown in the views in this work. It is certainly a most charming portion of the city, and an ideal spot for a home.

RESIDENCE OF T. W. BAXTER.

RESIDENCE OF S. M. INMAN, ATLANTA.

FROM DRAWING.   L. B. WHEELER and W. T. DOWNING, Architects.

RESIDENCE OF J. W. RANKIN, CAPITAL AVENUE.

RESIDENCE OF CAPTAIN ISAAC S. BOYD, PEACHTREE STREET.

RESIDENCE AT INMAN PARK.

Residence of P. H. Harralson Esq,
Inman Park   Atlanta Ga,

A. M. Young Arch't
Atlanta Ga.

RESIDENCE OF P. H. HARRALSON, INMAN PARK.

ANNOTATIONS

Page 1: *Lake Abana. After it was drained many years ago, the site was used as a barnyard museum for domestic animals and fowl.*

Page 2: *(top) Looking northwest (right) and southwest (left). Collins and Calhoun streets are now known as Courtland Street and Piedmont Avenue. The photograph was taken from the place where the Marriott Hotel now stands.*

(bottom, left) Peachtree Street looking north. Site to the right is now Plaza Park, over railroad tracks; to left is the present First National Bank building.

(bottom, right) Looking west. Georgia Railroad roundhouse, south of the tracks between the present-day Washington Street bridge and Piedmont Avenue. The cupola (upper left) topped Fire Engine House #2, on Washington Street.

Page 3: *Looking northwest from the State Capitol dome. Central Presbyterian Church is in the lower left corner, and the clock tower was on the old Fulton County Courthouse at Pryor and Hunter (now Martin Luther King, Jr., Drive) streets.*

Page 6: *On the block bounded by Pryor, Decatur, and Wall streets, immediately south of Five Points. Now a site of small retail businesses and an indoor parking facility. Depicted here is the second Kimball House, built in 1885 and razed in 1959; the first Kimball House burned in 1883 at the same location.*

Page 7: *(top) West side of Peachtree Street looking north from Ellis Street. Today this is the site of Macy's department store.*

(bottom) Northwest corner of Peachtree and Ellis streets, also now Macy's department store. Atlanta's oldest private club (founded in 1883), its location in 1986 is 7 Harris Street, N.W., two blocks north.

Page 8: *(top) Looking south on what is now Peachtree Street, S.W., from Hunter Street, now Martin Luther King, Jr., Drive, then Atlanta's chief retail shopping center.*

(bottom) Looking southeast from Broad Street bridge, with the new Kimball House on the left. The depot was demolished in 1929 to make way for a new station facing Forsyth Street. Site is now part of Plaza Park.

Page 10: *(top) Hill, a lawyer, was active in politics, serving terms in both the state legislature and the United States Congress. The statue faced south at the junction of Peachtree and West Peachtree streets. It now stands in the State Capitol.*

(bottom) Built in 1883 at what is now the southeast corner of Piedmont and Ponce de Leon avenues. The building still exists as a restaurant called The Mansion. Edward Peters was a real estate developer, alderman, banker, and the son of prominent pioneer Atlantan Richard Peters.

Page 11: *(2) Intersection of Peachtree and Kimball streets (now Ponce de Leon Avenue), looking toward the present Fox Theatre.*

(3) Southwest corner Peachtree and Cain (now International Boulevard) streets, now site of the Peachtree Plaza Hotel.

(4) West side, looking north from Ellis Street.

(5) Inman Park, in the process of development.

Page 13: *(top) Looking southeast at Five Points, with Edgewood Avenue to the left and Decatur Street to the right. At left is the artesian well described on page 37.*

(bottom) Looking east toward Loyd Street (now Central Avenue). In the distance is the Markham House hotel, in front of which President Grover Cleveland spoke on 18 October 1887. The site of the Markham is now part of Georgia State University. Union Station is to the right.

Page 14: *(top) West side, between Linden and North avenues. Hemphill, Sr., was mayor of Atlanta, business manager of the Constitution Publishing Co., and president of the Atlanta Trust & Banking Co.*

(bottom) South side of Ponce de Leon Avenue between Juniper Street and Piedmont Avenue. Knowles was an insurance executive.

Page 15: *Joel Hurt began developing this area in 1888.*

Page 16: *Gould Building on Decatur Street just east of Five Points.*

Page 18: *(top) Now southeast corner of the park at Boulevard and Atlanta Avenue. Named for Confederate general W. H. T. Walker, the fort was one of a series of such defenses encircling Atlanta in 1864.*

(bottom) East side of Washington Street between Love and Little streets south of Atlanta-Fulton County Stadium. Demolished in 1974. The architect was Gottfried L. Norrman [sic]. Now site of Our Lady of Perpetual Help Cancer Clinic.

Page 19: *East side of West Peachtree Street just south of Linden Avenue near Crawford W. Long Memorial Hospital. Hoke Smith served as secretary of the interior, 1893-1896; governor of Georgia, 1907-1909; and U.S. senator, 1911-1921.*

Page 20: *Northeast side of Marietta Street just southeast of North Avenue. Now site of The Coca-Cola Company headquarters.*

Page 22: *(top) West side, between Cedar (now Alexander) and Pine streets. Now a parking lot. Cabaniss was business manager of the* Atlanta Evening Journal *and president of the Georgia Security and Banking Co. E. P. Black was freight agent for the Western and Atlantic Railroad.*

Page 23: *Factory was at Tennels (now Tenelle) and Borne (now Powell) streets just south of the Georgia Railroad (now Seaboard) and east of the Fulton Cotton Mills, now closed. See pages 35 and 78.*

Page 24: *(top) North side of Gordon, now site of Howell Park. Howell was the managing editor of the* Atlanta Constitution.
(bottom) North side of Gordon between Ashby and Peeples streets, at residence of Evan P. Howell. Present site of Howell Park. In 1890 Howell was president of the Constitution Publishing Co. and editor-in-chief of the Atlanta Constitution. *See page 32.*

Page 25: *Georgia State Capitol, north side, second floor. The library is now housed in the state judicial building.*

Page 27: *Southeast corner of Hunter (now Martin Luther King, Jr., Drive) and Whitehall (now Peachtree Street, S.W.) streets. Now a parking lot. The company sold dry goods, clothing, and furniture. The building was later occupied by J. M. High department store. Chamberlin's home appears on page 57.*

Page 28: *West side of Ashby Street between Park and Oak streets.*

Page 29: *The area between Berne Street and Confederate Avenue east of Boulevard in the Ormwood Park area was called Little Switzerland. The site is now covered with kudzu.*

Page 31: *(1) Looking south from Decatur Street, with the 1885 Kimball House, demolished in 1959, in the foreground to the right on the southwest corner of Pryor and Decatur streets.*
(2) Probably southwest Atlanta, between West End and Fort McPherson.
(3) Between Edgewood and Euclid avenues.
(4) More commonly known as the Gate City National Bank building and later called the Temple Court Building, it was located at the southwest corner of Alabama and Pryor streets. Lodowick J. Hill was president.
(5) Looking south. On the southwest corner is the Fitten Building, present site of the First Federal Savings and Loan Association.
(6) Looking west. The large central spire is part of Girl's High School, which was demolished in 1929. Girl's High was originally the John Neal residence, built in 1859. It stood on the grounds of the present City Hall and in the fall of 1864 was used as General Sherman's headquarters.

Page 32: *North side of Gordon Street between Ashby and Peeples streets in West End, present site of Howell Park.*

Page 33: *(top) Northwest corner of Forsyth and Luckie streets, later site of the Forsyth Building and now a parking lot. W. Wallace Boyd was secretary and treasurer of the Van Winkle Gin & Machinery Co.*
(bottom) Looking west from Peachtree Street (that is, from Five Points). To the far left in the Norcross Building is Jacob's Pharmacy where Coca-Cola was first sold in 1886 (note sign in lower left-hand corner). Now site of the First National Bank building.

Page 35: *(top) See page 23.*
(bottom) Northeast corner of Hunter (now Martin Luther King,

Jr., Drive) *and Butler streets, just east of the State Capitol. Swift's manufactured a "medicinal tonic."*

Page 36: *East side, between Peters (now Trinity Avenue) and Fair (now Memorial Drive) streets. Neal was president of the Neal Loan and Banking Co.*

Page 38: *Later known as the Murray Company, it was located in northwest Atlanta at Howell Station near Howell Mill Road and what is now the Hemphill Pumping Station of the Atlanta Water Works, approximately three miles from Five Points. It is presently the site of the Murray Hill complex, which still uses some of the original Van Winkle buildings.*

Page 39: *Northeast corner of West Peachtree and Third streets. Present site of several small retail businesses. Edward Van Winkle was president of Van Winkle Gin & Machinery Co. See page 38.*

Page 40: *On line of the Western & Atlantic Railroad (now Seaboard) and Eastern Tennessee, Virginia, and Georgia Railroad (now Southern) a short distance northwest of what are now Southern Railway Inman Yard and Seaboard's Tilford Yard off Marietta Road in Northwest Atlanta. In 1890 the office and retail store of the Cooledge firm were located at 21 East Alabama Street, south side, between Whitehall (now Peachtree Street, S.W.) and Pryor streets.*

Page 44: *Southeast corner of Alabama and Forsyth streets. Demolished in 1967 for an expansion of Rich's department store.*

Page 45: *Southeast corner of Pryor (now Park Place) and Wheat (now Auburn Avenue) streets. Looking east on Wheat, now site of the Trust Company bank. After 1914 the building was known as the Chamber of Commerce Building.*

Page 48: *Northwest corner of Washington and Rawson streets, now site of the downtown interchange. Brown was a prominent lawyer and civic leader, son of Joseph E. Brown, Georgia's Civil War governor, and brother of Joseph M. Brown, governor of Georgia 1909-1911.*

Page 49: *(top) First two buildings of Georgia Institute of Technology. To the left is the shops building, destroyed by fire in 1892. The administration building to the right still stands.*
(bottom) Looking west from West Peachtree Street on Hunnicutt, which was soon changed to Baltimore Block. Center, facing Spring Street, is the former Calvin W. Hunnicutt home.

Page 50: *Looking west near the intersection of Pryor and Alabama streets. The building to the left is the Gate City National Bank, later the Temple Court Building. See page 31.*

Page 51: *Hunter Street (now Martin Luther King, Jr., Drive) is to the right of the clock tower. Now part of the Morris Brown College campus.*

Page 53: *Intersection of Ellis and Church (now Carnegie Way) streets, now site of Macy's department store, Carnegie Way entrance.*

Page 54: *Originally built at the intersection of McDonough Boulevard and Capitol Avenue, the school later became part of the Atlanta University Center. Its site is 653 Beckwith Street, S.W., where the school moved in 1962. Founded in 1883 as* the Gammon School of Theology, a unit of Clark University, it is affiliated with the United Methodist Church and is now known as Interdenominational Theological Center. Faculty homes were part of the campus. Gammon Hall was a dormitory.

Page 55: Founded in 1890 at McDonough Boulevard near Capitol Avenue. The name of the school was changed in 1940 to Clark College, after its incorporation into the Atlanta University Center. Warren Hall was a women's dormitory. The trade school's curriculum, for men only, included farming, painting, wagon and carriage making, carpentry, and wheelwrighting. Instruction in housekeeping was offered to women in the "model home." Chrisman Hall housed classrooms, a chapel, and dormitory facilities. The college moved to Chestnut Street, S.W., in 1941.

Page 56: (top) Located immediately north of the Winship Machine Co. (see page 64) between Thurmond and what is now Fuller streets. Incorporated in 1856, the company in 1986 holds the distinction of being the oldest incorporated business still in existence in Atlanta. Now location of the Georgia World Congress Center.

(bottom) On the west side of the "old Monroe" tracks at the southeast corner of Rhodes and Hulsey streets, now site of the Omni MARTA station. The Atlanta and Gate City gas companies had the same office address and the same manager, W. G. Abel.

Page 57: (top) The site is near the Garnett Street MARTA station and is now surrounded by government offices. Edward Payson Chamberlin was a partner in one of Atlanta's leading dry goods stores, Chamberlin, Johnson & Co., in the 1890s and later. See page 27.

(bottom) Just south of Simpson Street between Vine and Arthur (now Sunset Avenue) streets, and now a Georgia Power substation.

Page 59: In the old Capitol building, northwest corner of Marietta and Forsyth streets. Now site of Western Union building.

Page 60: (1) Located at northwest corner of Walton and Forsyth streets, where the old post office now stands.

(2) Central Presbyterian (foreground) still stands.

(3) Site of the first church in Atlanta (1847), Wesley Chapel, at the junction of Peachtree, Houston, and Pryor streets. The church was razed to make way for the Candler Building in 1903.

(4) Looking southeast from Spring Street. To the right is First Presbyterian Church, built in 1878 and demolished in 1919. To the right of the church is the John Silvey house, now site of the Federal Reserve Bank.

(5) On the southwest corner of East Peters Street, later Trinity Avenue, and Whitehall Street, S.W., now Peachtree Street. The church stood across the street from the E. P. Chamberlin residence. See page 57.

Page 61: South side of Georgia Railroad tracks at Clifton Road. The works were in the DeKalb County community of Edgewood, two-and-a-half miles east of Atlanta. Gossypium is the Latin name for the genus of plants commonly known as cotton. Residue from cottonseed is used not only in the manufacture of fertilizer but also for livestock feed, photographic film, and explosives.

Page 62: (top) Built in 1890 at the northwest corner of Pryor and Hunter streets, now Martin Luther King, Jr., Drive. Presently a parking lot, the site is diagonally across the street and to the north of the Fulton County Courthouse on the southwest fringe of the Underground Atlanta Historic and Cultural Conservation District.

(bottom) Northeast corner of Hunter (now Martin Luther King, Jr., Drive) and Washington streets. Present site of the Georgia Department of Agriculture. In 1933 the board of trustees voted to sell the Hunter Street property and move the cathedral to Andrews Drive and Peachtree Street, its present location.

Page 63: Northwest corner of Pryor Street (now Park Place) and Edgewood Avenue. Demolished in 1974. Moore & Marsh were wholesale dry goods merchants. Now the Robert W. Woodruff Park, southeast corner.

Page 64: (top) West side of the Western & Atlantic Railroad tracks just north of Magnolia Street, now International Boulevard. The company manufactured guns for the Confederacy. The shops were destroyed by General Sherman's troops in 1864, but the company was rebuilt and merged with the Continental Gin Co. in 1900 to become a world leader in the production of cotton gins. Robert Winship, one of the owners, was the maternal grandfather of Atlanta philanthropist Robert Winship Woodruff. Site of the Georgia World Congress Center.

(bottom) Intersection of Humphries and Glenn streets, S.W. The area lies between Mechanicsville and West End near the Southern Railway main line to Macon, a short distance north of the Southern Railway Pegram Shops, formerly known as South Shops.

Page 66: (top) Marietta Street between North Avenue and Means Street. This site is just west of the Georgia Tech campus, where North Avenue passes under the multiple Southern and Seaboard railroad tracks.

(bottom) Northwest corner. The Brown & King Supply Co. sold mill supplies, machinery, and tools. Now site of Rich's department store.

Page 67: (top) West side of Richmond and Danville Railroad (now Southern Railway belt line) between Irwin Street and Edgewood Avenue.

(bottom) Manufacturers of plows. The works, on the west side of Marietta Street between Jones Avenue and Mills Street, ran back to the Richmond & Danville (now Southern Railroad) tracks.

Page 68: (top) South of North Avenue.

(bottom) Present location of Southern Railway Pegram Shops. Between Windsor Street, S.W., and Southern Railway main line to Macon.

Page 69: On Marietta Street just beyond Mayson and Turner Road, now Bankhead Avenue. Between the railroad tracks and Marietta Street, the site is a short distance west of the Georgia Tech campus and is now set aside for commercial and light industrial uses.

Page 70: *(top) Intersection of McPherson and Monument avenues, East Atlanta.*

(bottom) Near intersection of Harden and Jones (now Woodward Avenue) streets, one block southwest of Oakland Cemetery.

Page 72: *East side of Pryor Street (now Park Place) between Wheat Street (now Auburn Avenue) and Houston Street, just northeast of Robert W. Woodruff Park.*

Page 73: *(left) Northeast corner, now the northern perimeter of Underground Atlanta. Wellhouse & Sons manufactured paper products.*

(right) At intersection of Clarke Street, just north of the Atlanta-Fulton County Stadium. Scott was a real estate agent.

Page 75: *(top) Founded in 1881 as the Atlanta Baptist Female Seminary, the school's name was changed in 1884 to Spelman College in honor of Mrs. John D. Rockefeller's mother, Mrs. Harvey Spelman. Mr. Rockefeller had made several substantial financial gifts to the college. Packard Hall was named for a school founder, Sophia B. Packard. In 1929 the school became a unit of the Atlanta University Center.*

(bottom) The forerunner of Morehouse College, it was founded in 1867 as the Augusta Institute and moved to Atlanta in 1879. This is Graves Hall, built in 1889 at what was the west end of Fair Street, on the western edge of the present Morehouse campus.

Page 76: *(top) West side of Hill Street, S.E., between Logan Street and Glenwood Avenue. Interstate 20 passes under this site. The home is no longer standing. John J. Falvey was proprietor of J. J. Falvey & Co., produce merchants.*

(bottom) Collins was president of the Atlanta Exchange and Banking Co. His residence was on Marietta Road, beyond city limits, at Bolton.

Page 77: *(top) Southeast corner, Gilmer and Butler streets, near Grady Memorial Hospital.*

(bottom) Near the northwest corner of Mangum and Markham streets, a short distance west of Southern Railway buildings.

Page 78: *See page 23.*

Page 79: *Southwest corner of West Peachtree and Fifth streets, later site of Capital Automobile Co. Rice was vice president, Atlanta Exchange and Banking Co.*

Page 80: *West side of Peachtree between Ellis and Cain (now International Boulevard) streets. Site today is part of Macy's department store. Mrs. Richards was the widow of Robert H. Richards, vice-president of the Atlanta National Bank.*

Page 81: *(top) Inman Park. Goodrich was an architect and builder.*

(bottom) Southwest corner, presently part of Rich's garage.

Page 82: *(top) Between present Myrtle Street and Argonne Avenue, also known as "Little Tyrol" park. Hartman was a florist of Swiss descent. According to one account, the park was lovely, but the area was also used to carry off Atlanta sewage.*

(bottom) Southeast corner of Cone and Poplar streets. The house faced Cone.

Page 83: *(top) West Fourth Street near Marietta Street. Site is now part of Georgia Tech.*

(bottom) Marietta and Wallace streets, now part of the site of Randall Bros. Company offices were on Broad Street, just northeast of Marietta Street.

Page 86: *West side of Spring Street between Harris and Cain (now International Boulevard) streets, opposite the Merchandise Mart. Now site of the Diplomat restaurant.*

Page 87: *Southwest corner, Peachtree Street and Ponce de Leon Avenue. Samuel Inman was senior partner in S. M. Inman & Co., the largest cotton merchants in the South. He was called Atlanta's first citizen for his substantial civic and philanthropic contributions.*

Page 88: *Northwest corner of Fulton Street. Present site of Fulton County Juvenile Court, just north of Atlanta-Fulton County Stadium.*

Page 89: *Southeast corner of Peachtree and Sixth streets, now site of a parking lot. I. S. Boyd was a partner in Boyd & Baxter Furniture Co. See page 69.*

Page 91: *South side of Edgewood Avenue between Waddell and Spruce streets. Phillip H. Harralson was one of the proprietors of Harralson Brothers & Co., wholesale tobacco merchants.*

INDEX